# The Delawares

BIBLIOGRAPHICAL SERIES
*The Newberry Library Center
for the History of the American Indian*

*General Editor*
Francis Jennings


*The Center Is Supported by Grants from*

The National Endowment for the Humanities
The Ford Foundation
The W. Clement and Jessie V. Stone Foundation
The Woods Charitable Fund, Inc.

# The Delawares

*A Critical Bibliography*

## C. A. WESLAGER

Published for the Newberry Library

*Indiana University Press*

BLOOMINGTON AND LONDON

Library of Congress Cataloging in Publication Data
Weslager, Clinton Alfred, 1909–
The Delawares.
(Bibliographical series)
Includes index.
1. Delaware Indians—Bibliography. I. Title.
II. Series.
Z1210.D4W47    [E99.D2]    016.97'0004'97    78-3250
ISBN 0-253-31680-4    1 2 3 4 5 82 81 80 79 78

# CONTENTS

## RECOMMENDED WORKS

### For the Beginner

[9]    Sonia Bleeker, *The Delaware Indians*.

[23]   Jane Levis Carter, *The Down River People of the Leni-Lenape Indians*.

[60]   Mark R. Harrington, "The Life of a Lenape Boy."

[61]   Mark R. Harrington, *Dickon among the Indians*.

[160]  Frank G. Speck, "Cruising the Eastern Woods with a Delaware Chief."

[203]  C. A. Weslager, *A Brief Account of the Indians of Delaware*.

### For a Basic Library Collection

[25]   Dorothy Cross, *New Jersey's Indians*.

[45]   Lawrence Henry Gipson, ed., *The Moravian Mission on White River*.

[59]   Mark R. Harrington, *Religion and Ceremonies of the Lenape*.

[84]   Francis P. Jennings, "The Scandalous Indian Policy of William Penn's Sons: Deeds and Documents of the Walking Purchase."

[97]   Herbert C. Kraft, ed., *A Delaware Indian Symposium*.

# BIBLIOGRAPHICAL ESSAY

## Introduction

The Delaware Indians were members of an Algonkian-speaking tribe who called themselves the Lenape or Lenni Lenape. The word *Lenape* standing alone means "common people," and the addition of *Lenni*, although redundant, reinforces this meaning. Delaware is not an Indian word but is derived from the name of Thomas West, Lord de la Warr, one of the early governors of the Virginia colony. Lord de la Warr's name was given to a bay and a river and later was modified to Delaware.

The heart of the Lenape homeland was the area that is now southeastern Pennsylvania, southeastern New York, and the states of Delaware and New Jersey. De la Warr's name became attached to the Lenape tribe at an early date; earlier still, they were known to many other tribes as "grandfathers," as discussed by Frank G. Speck, "The Wapanachki Delawares and the English: Their Past as Viewed by an Ethnologist" [158]. Speck points out they merited seniority and respect because Wapanachki, with its numerous variants ( Wabanaki, Wabanocky, Abnaki, etc.), denotes "Sunrise Land" or "Easterners." According to Speck, this suggests that the Delawares were the original occupants to come eastward to the land nearest the rising sun. Hence they were considered venerated grandfathers.

One of the problems in reconstructing the history and customs of the Delawares is that the tribe no longer lives in its original homeland. The influx of White settlers during the colonial period forced them to leave their native villages and go west to find new homes, and Delaware descendants may be found today in forty-six states, as well as in Canada. The story of their westward migrations and their settlements en route is told in some of the books and articles listed in the bibliography.

This bibliography is not intended to be exhaustive; space limitations have required me to be selective. Some titles were published in obscure sources. For instance, a publication called the *American Antiquarian and Oriental Journal* contained articles about the Delawares as early as 1879; but these titles have been omitted, as have some others, because the publications are hard to find.

Manuscript references have also been omitted. Among these are the Grant Foreman Collection in the Oklahoma Historical Society Library; the Richard Graham Papers in the Missouri Historical Society Library; the Burton Collection in the Detroit Public Library; the Archives of the Moravian Church; and the voluminous records of the Bureau of Indian Affairs in the National Archives and Records Service. The field notes of scientists who investigated the Delawares earlier in this century also contain useful data. Among these are the notes of Frank G. Speck in the Delaware Indian manuscript collections of the American Philosophical Society; the field notes of Mark R. Harrington in the files of the Museum of the American Indian, Heye Foundation; and those of Truman Michelson in the Smithsonian Institution.

In the future it is likely that scholars sifting through these and other manuscripts will find material worthy of publication that will add new studies to the literature of the Delaware tribe. Ethnohistorians currently working with Delaware Indian traditionalists may obtain new information for use in books and articles. In the meantime, plenty of interesting and informative accounts are now available.

A basic reference is C. A. Weslager, *The Delaware Indians: A History* [213]. Another general, but incomplete account is Richard C. Adams, "A Brief History of the Delaware Indians" [3]. Adams, who was part Delaware, represented the tribe in Washington, D.C., for about twenty-five years, and he wrote from an Indian viewpoint. Adams was the author of at least twelve articles, but space permits listing only three of them.

The *Handbook of American Indians North of Mexico*, edited by Frederick Webb Hodge [70], was for many years considered the authoritative Indian encyclopedia. See the entries under "Delaware" in volume 1, pages 385–87, "Walam Olum" in volume 2, page 898, and others under individual names of chiefs and villages. However, some of this material is now outdated and should be checked against other sources. A new edition of the *Handbook*, now being prepared, will soon be issued by the Smithsonian Institution.

Weslager, "The Indians of Delaware" [140, chap. 2], gives a short account of the history of the Delaware tribe.

A more technical treatise is *The Culture and Acculturation of the Delaware Indians*, by William W. Newcomb, Jr. [127], which deals primarily with changes that took place in Delaware culture as a result of years of White contact. Newcomb, an anthropologist, conducted an ethnographic study among the Delawares in Oklahoma in 1951 and 1952, and his analysis of how they assimilated the customs of the Whites at the expense of their own culture is well presented. The weakness of the volume is Newcomb's comments on the names and locations of the Delaware villages when the tribe lived in the East.

Vernon Kinietz, in *Delaware Culture Chronology* [96], also tried to determine what changes took place in Delaware culture, and why. He attempted to compile a trait list of data recorded by others in the seventeenth, eighteenth, and nineteenth centuries, but the study is imprecise and lacks validity. His six-page "Historical Sketch" preceding the cultural analysis is an inadequate summary of Delaware tribal history.

**Where Did the Delawares Come From?**

The Delaware Indians had no formal system of reading and writing before the coming of the White man, and lacking an alphabet they had no written histories to explain their origins. They did use a primitive system of communication by scratching or cutting stick figures and symbols on stone or wood or painting figures on the bark of trees or on wood tablets. In *The Lenape Stone; or, The Indian and the Mammoth*, Henry C. Mercer [110] illustrates and discusses a stone gorget perforated with two holes and incised with the likeness of an animal that appeared to be a hairy mammoth. It was plowed up in Bucks County, Pennsylvanis, in 1872, but its being found in an area occupied by Delawares in the seventeenth century does not necessarily mean it was made by a Delaware Indian, as Mercer surmised.

Throughout the area where the Delawares lived, etched stone ornaments have been found, as well as pictures called petroglyphs, inscribed on large stones and rocks. Stone artifacts cut in the likeness of human faces have also been found; see Charles A. Philhower, *The Human Face in Lenape Archeology* [135], and Alanson Skinner, "Two Lenape Stone Masks from Pennsylvania and New Jersey" [151].

The most controversial pictorial representation is the Walam Olum, which means "red score" or "painted record," a series of small flat sticks or tablets on which symbols were painted in red. Each stick might be compared to a page in a book, and in *Dickon among the Indians* [61] — a fictional account based on factual data — Mark R. Harrington describes how certain Indian patriarchs were taught to interpret the meaning of the pictures. The Walam Olum supposedly tells the story of the Delawares from the Creation to the coming of the White man. No one knows what became of the inscribed sticks. An eccentric scholar named Constantine Rafinesque claimed that he saw the inscribed sticks in 1822 and copied the pictures and that he also obtained the Indian words that explained their meanings.

After Rafinesque's death, a Philadelphia physician, Daniel G. Brinton, who became a professor of American linguistics and archeology at the University of Pennsylvania, redrew the pictures from Rafinesque's copies and reproduced them with a new translation of the Indian words in *The Lenape and Their Legends, with the Complete Text and Symbols of the Walam Olum* [14].

Although Brinton was a capable scholar, his book contains a number of errors. He refers to the Reverend John Campanius as Thomas, who was the minister's grandson. Weslager and Arthur R. Dunlap challenged Brinton's statements that a place in the state of Delaware was known to the Delawares as Walamink ("the place of paint") and that there was an Indian village near Wilmington called Chikahokin; see their *Indian Place-Names in Delaware* [202, pp. 49, 53].

The original pictures copied by Rafinesque and a new English translation of the Indian words were published in *Walam Olum, or Red Score: The Migration Legend of the Lenni Lenape or Delaware Indians*, written jointly by Glenn A. Black, Eli Lilly, Georg K. Neumann, Joe E. Pierce, Charles F. Voegelin, Erminie W. Voegelin, and Paul Weer [184]. This volume reveals (p. xiii) that Brinton copied one of Rafinesque's pictures upside down and that fifty eight differences were found between Brinton's and Rafinesque's drawings. According to the interpretations made there, the Delawares came to Alaska from Asia across the Bering Strait (not from Labrador as Brinton believed), and then went south to the Mississippi River. There they engaged in a war with the Talligewi tribe, after which they continued their journey to the East.

Authorities who distrusted Rafinesque have debated whether the Walam Olum is genuine or a fraud. William

W. Newcomb, Jr., states in "The Walam Olum of the Delaware Indians in Perspective" [124] that it is difficult to accept Rafinesque's pictures as an authentic account of the Delaware migrations and that archeological evidence is lacking to support his account. He does not deny that the pictures may have been drawn originally by a Delaware Indian, but he believes they may have been made between 1750 and 1812, at the time the tribe was reviving native legends to counteract the influence of the White man's culture. Newcomb believes the Walam Olum would be a logical accompaniment to a revivalist movement when Delaware traditionalists were trying to keep nativism alive. This is an interesting and plausible theory, but it is unproved.

Erminie W. Voegelin introduces evidence in "Culture Parallels to the Delaware Walam Olum" [180] that other eastern tribes preserved the story of their past by pictographs painted on sticks and that there is little reason to doubt the authenticity of the Walam Olum.

## Seventeenth-century Accounts

Knowledge of the early history and culture of the Delaware Indians is based on reports, letters, and journals written by travelers, settlers, and missionaries; on old land records; on entries made in provincial archives; and on information obtained from Delaware descendants, passed down to them orally by their ancestors.

The Dutch, Swedes, Finns, and English, who were the first Europeans to come into contact with the Delawares, starting about A.D. 1600, had little interest in studying Indian culture. They considered the Indians heathens and savages when measured against European life-styles and traditions. Consequently the seventeenth-century written accounts are frequently inaccurate, often misleading, and usually incomplete. Later historians repeated the errors of their predecessors.

Many questions about the Delawares must remain unanswered, although useful information can be obtained by carefully studying the early records and allowing for the prejudices of the Europeans. Albert Cook Myers, *Narratives of Early Pennsylvania, West New Jersey and Delaware 1630–1707* [120], collected representative contemporary accounts relating to the Delawares written by David Pietersz. de Vries (1630–33; 1643) and Thomas Yong (1634); two reports by Governor Johan Printz (1644–45); two reports by Governor Johan Rising (1655); a description of Pennsylvania and New Jersey by Gabriel Thomas (1689); and the observations of William Penn and other Europeans.

Myers later published *William Penn His Own Account of the Lenni Lenape or Delaware Indians, 1683* [121], including Penn's letter to the Free Society of Traders. Myers included reproductions of contemporary Delaware Indian deeds and photographs of historical markers placed on the sites of three former Delaware towns in Pennsylvania and Delaware: Playwicky, Minguannan, and Queonomysing. Dunlap and Weslager discussed the latter town on Brandywine Creek in "Two Delaware Valley Indian Place-Names" [35]. Myers also included several of Penn's letters pertaining to the Delaware and Penn's description (pp. 55–57) of a Delaware taking a sweat bath. His illustrations included reproductions of portraits of two Delaware chiefs, Lappawinzo and Tishcohan, painted by order of John Penn in 1735. Further details about these two rare paintings by the Swedish artist Gustav Hesselius can be found in "Lappawinzo and Tishcohan," by William J. Buck [19]. These are the only existing portraits of early Delaware chiefs.

In *The Instruction for Johan Printz*, Amandus Johnson [87] translated into English the orders given Printz in 1642 when he left Sweden for America to govern the colony on the Delaware River. Printz was instructed how he should treat the Indians to win their friendship and support. The volume also contains Johnson's translations of letters and reports that Printz sent back to Sweden after his arrival in America. These communications indicate that the Swedes were interested in three things: acquiring land from the Delawares, obtaining animal pelts from them, and converting them to Christianity, as Weslager emphasized in "The Swede Meets the Red Man" [208].

One of the most informative seventeenth-century accounts is Peter Lindeström's *Geographia Americae: With an Account of the Delaware Indians* [101]. Based on a journal Lindeström made in New Sweden in 1654–56, Johnson's English translation gives faithful descriptions of how the Delawares lived: their clothing, housing, ornaments, food, hunting and fishing practices, and other customs. The volume contains facsimiles of two maps drawn by Lindeström that give the native names of Indian villages and other places in the Delaware Valley. Weslager further developed this information in two accounts written for general readers: "Delaware Indian Villages" [196] and "Delaware Indian Villages at Philadelphia" [207]. Johnson appended a list of the meanings of the Indian geographical names shown on Lindeström's maps, but one must be wary about accepting his translations because he was not an authority on the Algonkian language, although his English translation of Lindeström's Swedish text is beyond reproach.

Another useful contemporary English translation is *A Short Description of the Province of New Sweden Now Called by the English Pennsylvania in America*, by Thomas Campanius Holm [71]. (His surname was Campanius but he added Holm to it to indicate he was from Stockholm.) Although this work was not printed until 1702, it was inspired by a journal kept by the author's grandfather, the Reverend John (Johannes) Campanius, a Lutheran minister who accompanied Governor Printz to America. Thomas Campanius Holm never visited America, and his account is not as reliable as Lindeström's, which is based on personal observations. Nevertheless, Holmes had the advantage of using his grandfather's notes, and like his grandfather he concluded that the Indians were of Jewish origin ( William Penn made the same error). He is also guilty of exaggeration, as in his description of an American rattlesnake with a head as big as a dog's, which could bite off a man's leg "as if it had been hewn down with an axe" (p. 53).

During his sojourn in New Sweden, as reported by his grandson, the Reverend John Campanius toured the

Delaware villages in an attempt to convert the Indians, and he translated Martin Luther's *Catechism* into the Delaware dialect. Upon his return to Sweden he presented a manuscript copy of the translation to the king in 1656. It was published in 1696 under the title *Lutheri Catechismus* [22], the earliest religious tract to record the Delaware dialect. The Indian words are actually a sort of jargon, although the Delawares could apparently understand them when they were read aloud by a Swede. The *Catechism* also contains a Delaware Indian word list with Swedish translations, but this has never been translated into English.

Data about Delaware Indian customs are also given in translations of Dutch documents written by seventeenth-century explorers and settlers. John de Laet's "Extracts from the New World; or, A Description of the West Indies" [99], written in 1625, is one of the earliest Dutch accounts. A more authoritative source is David Pietersz. de Vries, "Voyages from Holland to America, A.D. 1632 to 1644" [30], and another is "A Description of the New Netherland," by Adriaen Van der Donck [175]. These journals do not treat exclusively of the Indians, but also contain references to Dutch-Indian relations. Chapter 4 of Weslager's *Dutch Explorers, Traders, and Settlers in the Delaware Valley 1606–1664* [210], based on de Vries's account, relates how the Delaware Indians massacred the Dutch settlers at Swanendael (present Lewes, Delaware). This volume also includes seventeenth-century documentary references to land the Dutch purchased from the Delawares.

A description of the early Delaware Indian communities in New Jersey is found in a letter written by an Englishman, Robert Evelyn, first published in 1641 in an anonymous tract and reprinted in 1648. Weslager uses the 1641 version in his transcription in "Robert Evelyn's Indian Tribes and Place-Names of New Albion" [205]. Evelyn's letter names nine Indian communities in New Albion, the designation for land in New Jersey patented to Sir Edmund Plowden. Weslager places these communities on a modern map with suggested interpretations of the Indian names.

"Toponomy of the Delaware Valley as Revealed by an Early Seventeenth Century Map," by Weslager and Dunlap [209], adds to the knowledge of the general location of these early autonomous Delaware Indian communities. A facsimile of a map accompanying the article is dated by the authors about 1629. This article, and Evelyn's letter, would be more useful if the authors had been able to pinpoint village locations and describe the dwellings and customs of the residents. Unfortunately, neither the map nor the letter provides these details. "More Missing Evidence: Two Depositions by Early Swedish Settlers," by Dunlap and Weslager [34], dated 1683–84, contains affidavits by two aged Swedes relative to the bounds of the lands purchased from the Delawares by Peter Minuit, leader of the first Swedish expedition.

Marshall Becker uncovered contemporary records pertaining to one of the smaller Delaware communities; see "The Okehocking: A Remnant Band of Delaware Indians" [8]. In *Red Men on the Brandywine*, Weslager [204] compiled documentary data about a band of Delawares who lived along Brandywine Creek in Pennsylvania and Delaware, with the names of their chiefs. Charles A. Philhower attempted a local study entitled "South Jersey Indians on the Bay, the Cape and the Coast," which appears in Frank H. Stewart, *Indians of Southern New Jersey* [162, pp. 24-47]. In the absence of thorough documentary research, much of the article deals in generalities.

Philhower's "The Historic Minisink Site" [137] and "The Indians of the Morris County Area in New Jersey" [136] are commendable efforts to characterize the Indians who lived above the Delaware Water Gap, but they lack depth of research in deeds and other primary sources.

Herbert C. Kraft, *The Minisink Settlements: An Investigation into a Prehistoric and Early Historic Site in Sussex County, New Jersey* [98], is an outstanding study of the Minisinks (later called Munsies or Munsees). Kraft is critical of Philhower's archeological work, and he does not agree that the Minisink wigwams were grouped together and surrounded by palisades. He believes the huts were not in close proximity to each other. This may apply to the Minisinks, but not to the Delawares proper, who, according to Lindeström in *Geographia Americae* [101, p. 170], "have their dwellings side by side one another."

The Indians of the upper Delaware region are also discussed in Vernon Leslie's *Faces in Clay* [100]. Leslie, a non professional archeologist and former editor of the *Pennsylvania Archaeologist,* has conducted extensive research in the Minisink country, where he has lived for many years.

D. B. Brunner, author of *The Indians of Berks County, Pa, Being a Summary of All the Tangible Records of the Aborigines of Berks County* [18], devotes about half of his 257-page text to early accounts of the Delawares and the other half to illustrations of prehistoric artifacts and the locations of farms where they were plowed up. Brunner, an educator and author of business textbooks, was an Indian hobbyist, but his book is an outdated mishmash of history and prehistory, and he fails to relate one to the other.

*The Down River People of the Lenni-Lenape Indians,* by Jane Levis Carter [23], covers the entire Delaware River area, with emphasis on Chester County, Pennsylvania. A reader can learn much about the Delawares from this thirty-nine page account based on reliable sources. Frank G. Speck's "Speaking of the Delawares" [154] is a transcript of a paper read before the New Jersey Archaeological Society that gives a good perspective of the tribe in nine pages. Weslager, "The Indians of Lewes, Delaware, and an Unpublished Indian Deed Dated June 7, 1659" [201], introduces documentary data indicating that Delaware influence extended southward to Cape Henlopen. He theorizes that an Indian village at Lewes was occupied by Unalachtigo Delawares.

Mark R. Harrington's "The Life of a Lenape Boy" [60 ] is a brief fictional account of a Delaware boy born in Pennsylvania. Harrington was an authority on the Delawares, and his description of native custom and dress is exact.

Sonia Bleeker, *The Delaware Indians* [9 ], is one of a series of children's books on various tribes. Some of her statements are without historical support, such as the reference to a Delaware Big House at Shackamaxon, which is pure imagination. She refers to "Tamanend" (Tamany) as "their great leader" who signed the Great Treaty with William Penn that was never broken by Indians or Whites. She also says that the Delawares arrived in Oklahoma in 1812, fifty-five years before they actually got there. Little harm is done by these inaccuracies, since her basic story of the Delawares is correct and the book is not intended for sophisticated readers.

Weslager's *A Brief Account of the Indians of Delaware* [203] covers the customs of the Nanticokes and Delawares, although the emphasis is on the latter. This is one of a series of University of Delaware Press historical publications intended for readers as young as twelve years of age.

Anthony F. C. Wallace, in "Some Psychological Characteristics of the Delaware Indians during the 17th and 18th Centuries" [188 ], undertakes to characterize Delaware psychological traits from a study of early accounts. Contemporary literature in this area is incomplete and contradictory, and although Wallace deserves credit for trying, his paper is inconclusive. Philhower, in "Some Personal Characteristics of the Lenape Indians" [133 ], adds little of consequence to the subject.

Carol Barnes, "Subsistence and Social Organization of the Delaware Indians: 1600" [6], reconfirms the obvious information that the Delawares subsisted by hunting, fishing, trapping, and planting. She argues that they did a little of each and were not primarily agriculturists as some writers have said. She might have added that as White demands for furs increased it upset the native economy, and Delaware males became principally hunters and trappers in order to obtain trade goods.

Regina Flannery, using an analytic method based on ethnological data, compares Delaware subsistence, social organization, and other cultural aspects with those of neighboring Algonkian tribes in *An Analysis of Coastal Algonquian Culture* [41]. This work, Miss Flannery's published doctoral dissertation, is intended primarily for scholars acquainted with the literature of the Eastern Woodland Indians.

The seventeenth (and eighteenth) century provincial records of Pennsylvania, New York, and Maryland are interspersed with numerous references to official negotiations with the Delawares and other tribes. These archival records must be read judiciously, because some provincial officials made the minutes of their conferences with the Indians suit their own purposes. These sources are of greater use to the scholar than to the average reader, since careful study is required to find and interpret the Indian references.

The published *Pennsylvania Archives,* especially volume 1 in the first series, edited by Samuel Hazard [131], contain many references to land purchases and other diplomatic negotiations with the Delawares. The majority of the documents cited in volume 5 of the second series were copied from *Documents Relative to the Colonial History of the State of New York*, general editor Edmund B.

O'Callaghan [129], especially volume 12, which covers the Dutch and English settlements in the Delaware Valley when the Delawares were still in occupancy. Regrettably, this volume was edited by Berthold Fernow, who was neither Dutch nor American. His English translations of Dutch documents are not trustworthy, and his transcripts of English records are often faulty. *Collections of the New-York Historical Society* 2nd series, volume 1 [128], contains important Indian references by early Dutch explorers, competently translated.

A more accurate translation by Charles T. Gehring of some of the papers Fernow mistranslated, along with faithful transcripts of English documents, may be found in *New York Historical Manuscripts,* volumes 20–21, *Delaware Papers* [44].

*The Minutes of the Provincial Council of Pennsylvania from the Organization to the Termination of the Proprietary Government* [130], also known as the *Colonial Records*, contain innumerable references to the Delawares for the reader willing to sift through the wordy texts of sixteen volumes, a laborious job that only a scholar is usually willing to undertake. These records are especially rich in the minutes of treaty conferences.

The published *Archives of Maryland* [107], particularly volume 3, edited by William Hand Browne, which contains transcripts of two treaties between Maryland and the Delaware Indians, 1661 and 1663 (pp. 431–33, 486), are of utmost reference value. In volume 19, page 520, another important entry is recorded in 1697 that states the Delawares were then tributary to the Senecas (one of

the Five Nations) and were also subjects of the Sus-
quehannocks, or Minquas, who lived on the Susquehanna River. Weslager discusses this relationship in
"The Minquas and Their Early Relations with the Delaware Indians" [197], and offers evidence that the Minquas defeated the Delawares.

Amandus Johnson, *The Swedish Settlements on the Delaware: Their History and Relation to the Indians, Dutch and
English, 1638–1664* [86], includes many references to the
Delawares. This monumental work is based on a body of
material gathered in Sweden, Holland, England, and
Finland and in many ways can be considered a primary
source.

Edward M. Ruttenber's much-quoted *History of the
Indian Tribes of Hudson's River* [146], an overrated source
of information, was published in 1872, based on limited
primary sources and secondary works of uneven quality.
Research conducted since 1872 indicates that Ruttenber's interpretations of Delaware clans, bands, and geographical subdivisions should be revised. One of his
more obvious errors is in citing authorities (n. 5, p. 45)
that the "Allegewi" (he means the Talligewi referred to
in the *Walam Olum*) were of Welsh origin!

*Indian Affairs in Colonial New York: The Seventeenth
Century*, by Allen W. Trelease [172], is a modern,
authoritative study. Trelease properly raises doubts that
the Minisinks were a subdivision of the Delawares. He
believes that the Delaware tribe was not really a tribe at all
until well along in the eighteenth century, and that at the
time of White contact it was fragmented into thirty to

forty autonomous communities. I fully concur with this conclusion.

*Indians in Pennsylvania* [193], by Paul A. W. Wallace, and *New Jersey's Indians*, by Dorothy Cross [25], are books for popular reading containing details about Delaware Indian life and customs. Both authors were professional scholars, and their descriptions of dress, houses, food and cooking, warfare, canoes, trails, and so forth, are authentic. In another volume, *Indian Paths of Pennsylvania*, Wallace [194] traces the routes of several hundred Delaware Indian trails, the aboriginal channels of trade. These trails evolved into bridle paths and wagon roads, and some eventually became modern motor highways. Paul A. W. Wallace was the father of Anthony F. C. Wallace, and both are considered authorities on the Delawares.

William Nelson, *The Indians of New Jersey: Their Origin and Development, Manners and Customs, Language, Religion and Government* [122], is also a worthy attempt to reconstruct the history of the Delawares while they were occupying New Jersey; it too is meant for popular reading. Nelson's *Personal Names of Indians of New Jersey* [123] contains many Indian names abstracted from early deeds and other documents. It would have greater value if the author had found a Delaware-speaker who could give the English meanings of those names that are translatable.

Alanson Skinner, in *The Indians of Greater New York* [150, pp. 48-69], includes an account of the "Customs of the Delawares." His remarks also need updating, but

he did his best with the limited source material available
to him in 1915. M. W. Herman, "A Reconstruction of
Aboriginal Delaware Culture from Contemporary
Sources" [65], is a more effective, if incomplete, ap-
proach to the same subject.

## Early Relations with Whites and with Other Tribes

The Delaware Indian concept of land tenure explained by William Christie MacLeod in "The Family
Hunting Territory and Lenape Political Organization"
[104] is  reinforced by concrete examples in Weslager's
"A Discussion of the Family Hunting Territory Question
in Delaware," an addendum to *Indian Land Sales in Delaware*, by Leon de Valinger, Jr. [29].

De Valinger restricted his study of Dutch, Swedish,
and English land purchases to the state of Delaware.
Other sources must be consulted for transcripts of deeds
and treaties between the Delawares and the governments
of Pennsylvania and New Jersey. *Penn's Treaty with the
Indians*, by Charles S. Keyser [95], discusses the "Great
Treaty" that Penn is believed to have negotiated with the
Delawares at Shackamaxon in November 1682 (made
famous in an inaccurate painting by Benjamin West that
shows Penn as a portly middle-aged gentleman instead of
a young man of thirty eight). Keyser also enumerates the
deeds that extinguished Indian title to their lands. *Indian
Treaties Printed by Benjamin Franklin, 1736–1762*, edited
by Julian P. Boyd  [12], includes transcripts of later
deeds and treaties.

The first recorded deed personally signed by William Penn is dated 23 June 1683. Albert Cook Myers includes a transcript in *William Penn His Own Account of the Lenape or Delaware Indians* [121, pp. 88–89]. Myers also published (pp. 68–71) a transcript of an earlier land conveyance dated 12 April 1682, negotiated by Penn's agent, William Markham, who preceded the founder to America. Tradition persists that Penn was present in 1682 as one of the parties to the unrecorded Indian treaty at Shackamaxon; see Peter S. DuPonceau and J. Francis Fisher, "A Memoir on the History of the Celebrated Treaty Made by William Penn with the Indians under the Elm Tree at Shackamaxon in the Year 1682" [36]; Frederick D. Stone, "Penn's Treaty with the Indians: Did It Take Place in 1682 or 1683?" [164]; and Roberts Vaux, "A Memoir of the Locality of the Great Treaty between William Penn and the Indian Natives in 1682" [176].

Although land acquisition meant a cessation of Indian ownership, Penn negotiated fairly with the natives. After his death in 1718, Pennsylvania's Indian policies changed. In "The Delaware Interregnum," Francis Jennings [82] shows how James Logan, secretary of the province, interfered with the right of the Delawares to choose their own chiefs. Logan and others tried to get rid of the last Delawares remaining in Pennsylvania by selling to White buyers land still legally owned by the Indians. Jennings brings this mistreatment into sharp focus in "Incident at Tulpehocken" [83] and in "The Scandalous Indian Policy of William Penn's Sons: Deeds and Documents of the Walking Purchase" [84]. These fully documented essays set a high standard of quality for Delaware Indian literature.

Charles Thomson, a contemporary whose sympathies were with the Indians, reveals the exploitation of the Delawares after Penn's death in *Causes of the Alienation of the Delaware and Shawanese Indians from the British Interest* [168]. Samuel Allinson, "Fragmentary History of the New Jersey Indians" [4], tells how the Delawares in New Jersey were dispossessed of their lands and how, a century after the arrival of the first Europeans, the Delawares were a tribe without a country.

In their relations with other tribes, as previously mentioned, the Delawares fell under the subjection of the Susquehannock Minquas. This overlordship can be inferred in an affidavit in Myers's *Narratives* [120, pp. 86–89], indicating that Minquas representatives were present when the Delawares made the first land sale to the Swedes in 1638; Myers also (pp. 37–49) quotes from Thomas Yong, who encountered Minquas war parties in the Delaware River basin in 1634. MacLeod [104] emphasizes that the Delawares claimed their land in the Delaware Valley by ownership and descent "and by appointment of the Minquas."

Bad relations also existed between the Delawares and the Five Nations Iroquois of New York State. In 1742 the Five Nations claimed they had defeated the Delawares in warfare, figuratively emasculated them, and reduced them to the status of noncombatant women. Weslager summarizes the historical data relating to this feminization in "The Delaware Indians as Women" [199] and in

"Further Light on the Delaware Indians as Women" [200].

Although Weslager contends that a defeat, subjection, and feminization actually occurred, Speck, in "The Delaware Indians as Women: Were the Original Pennsylvanians Politically Emasculated?" [161], expresses doubt. He believes two questions should be resolved: Were the Delawares reduced by conquest to political impotence? Or were they accorded social supremacy as honored matrons? It is easier to ask such questions than to provide conclusive answers. The assumption that the Iroquois made honored matrons of the Delawares was previously expressed by John Heckewelder, *History, Manners, and Customs of the Indian Nations Who Once Inhabited Pennsylvania and Neighbouring States* [64, pp. 56–66]. Heckewelder's evidence includes no documentary confirmation.

Jay Miller, "The Delawares as Women: A Symbolic Solution" [113], theorizes that the feminization was an example of a cultural process called transformation by which cultural features are reversed, segregated, or redefined by mutal agreement. Although a novel explanation, it too lacks confirmation in historical sources or corroboration by Indian informants. Charles A. Hanna, *The Wilderness Trail* [55, 1:101–108], has something to say about the feminization but adds nothing new; nevertheless, his work adds worthy information to early Delaware history.

Anthony F. C. Wallace, "Women, Land, and Society: Three Aspects of Aboriginal Delaware Life" [185], covers political relations between the Delawares and the Five Nations. Wallace also treats competently of Delaware land tenure and social organization, although he incorrectly indicates (p. 9) that Delaware matrons were chiefmakers. This may be true of the Iroquois, but an aging incumbent Delaware chief nominated a successor from among certain "royal families" (by matrilineal descent), and his nomination, after consideration, was confirmed or rejected by a vote of the council. Delaware females did not participate in the election process or in the political deliberations of the men. See Charles C. Trowbridge, *Account of Some of the Traditions, Manners and Customs of the Lenee Lenaupaa or Delaware Indians* [173]; also Weslager, *The Delaware Indians: A History* [213, pp. 63–64].

Two essays by Jennings should be carefully considered by scholars interested in Iroquois-Delaware-White relations: "The Constitutional Evolution of the Covenant Chain" [85] and "The Delaware Indians in the Covenant Chain," in *A Delaware Indian Symposium*, edited by Herbert C. Kraft [97, pp. 89–101]. The "Covenant Chain" was a symbolic structure by which certain Indian tribes (including the Delawares) were allied with the provincial governments of Massachusetts, Connecticut, Maryland, and Virginia.

### Where Did the Delawares Go?

The Delaware population was greatly reduced by contagious diseases, overindulgence in intoxicants, and White hostility. Dispossessed of their homeland, they went west to lands the Whites had not penetrated, settling first along the Susquehanna River. During and after the French and Indian War they moved to Western Pennsylvania and Ohio. In their movement through Pennsylvania they lived in various towns, as enumerated (along with Delaware Valley Indian names) in George P. Donehoo, *A History of the Indian Villages and Place Names in Pennsylvania with Numerous Historical Notes and References* [31]. C. Hale Sipe, *Indian Chiefs of Pennsylvania* [148], and Sipe's *The Indian Wars of Pennsylvania* [149] are exciting and accurate accounts of the Delawares during the French and Indian Wars, suitable for popular reading. Merle H. Deardorff locates the towns on the Allegheny River established by the migrant Delawares and Munsies in "Zeisberger's Allegheny River Indian Towns: 1767–1770" [27].

William A. Hunter, editor of "John Hays' Diary and Journal of 1760" [77], which deals with a visit to the Delaware towns on the upper Susquehanna, is also the author of "Victory at Kittanning" [78], which describes Colonel John Armstrong's destruction of the Delawares' largest village on the Allegheny River on 8 September 1756. Hunter's *Forts on the Pennsylvania Frontier, 1753–1758* [79] recounts many of the Delaware raids during the French and Indian War, when the tribe fought on the side of the French. Hunter's "The Ohio, the Indian's Land" [76] gives a description of the Delawares' move west from the Susquehanna to the Ohio and Allegheny Rivers. Anthony F. C. Wallace,

in *King of the Delawares: Teedyuscung 1700–1763* [187],
covers the activities of the Delawares during the war and
the peace negotiations in a splendid work that is much
more than the biography the title suggests.

Wallace gives Indian emissaries credit for participat-
ing in the negotiations that led to a cessation of hostilities,
whereas Francis Parkman, an eminent nineteenth-
century historian, was biased in his views and failed to
give the Delaware diplomatic representatives the credit
they deserved. For more on this subject the reader
should consult "A Vanishing Indian: Francis Parkman
versus His Sources," in which Jennings [81] calls
Parkman to task for his inaccuracies.

*George Croghan, Wilderness Diplomat*, by Nicholas B.
Wainwright [183], is a highly recommended account of
Sir William Johnson's deputy and his relations with the
Delawares both as a White ambassador and as an entre-
preneur in the fur trade.

The "Narrative of John Brickell's Capitivity among
the Delawares" [13], and Beverly W. Bond, Jr., "The
Captivity of Charles Stuart, 1755–1757" [11], are
revealing journals by Whites held captive in Delaware
towns. The "Journal of James Kenny, 1761–1763,"
edited by John W. Jordan [94], is an equally informative
contemporary account.

After the French and Indian War was over and it
was safe for missionaries to go west, the Reverend
David Jones visited the Delaware towns on the Mus-
kingum, as described in *A Journal of Two Visits Made to
Some Nations of Indians on the West Side of the River Ohio,*

*in the Years 1772 and 1773* [90]. An educated Indian visitor from the East, Hendrick Aupaumut, kept another valuable journal containing references to the Delawares, "A Narrative of an Embassy to the Western Indians" [5].

The Revolution broke out while the Delawares were living in Ohio. During this critical period both the American colonies and the English sought Delaware military support. A compilation of primary source material by Reuben G. Thwaites and Louise P. Kellogg, *Frontier Defense on the Upper Ohio, 1777–1778* [171], is a selection of pertinent documents with numerous references to the Delawares. In *The Revolution on the Upper Ohio, 1775–1777* [170], Thwaites and Kellogg provide interesting interpretations of data relating to the Delawares.

Using the Draper manuscripts in the collections of the State Historical Society of Wisconsin, Louise P. Kellogg edited two fine volumes, *Frontier Advance on the Upper Ohio, 1778–1779* [92] and *Frontier Retreat on the Upper Ohio, 1779–1781* [93]. No study of the role of the Delawares in the Revolution would be complete without consulting these sources. Randolph C. Downes, *Council Fires on the Upper Ohio* [32] is another excellent book dealing with the Delawares and other tribes during the Revolution.

On 17 September 1778 the Delawares signed a treaty of alliance with commissioners representing the thirteen American states. This covenant, called the first peace treaty that the United States negotiated with an Indian tribe, is cited verbatim in *Indian Affairs: Laws and Treaties*, edited by Charles J. Kappler [91; see 2:3–5]. Kappler's work contains transcripts of all Indian treaties with the United States, including the subsequent treaties with the Delawares. Background information leading up to the Treaty of 1778 is found in David I. Bushnell, Jr., "The Virginia Frontier in History, 1778" [20], with specific references to White Eyes, Killbuck, and Captain Pipe, the Delaware signatories.

At the close of the Revolution, pressure from the advance of White settlers into Ohio forced the Delawares to move to Indiana Territory. As the main body consolidated in Indiana, splinter groups separated and moved north into Canada. Their descendants are living today at three locations in Ontario: Moraviantown on the Thames River between Bothwell and Thamesville; Muncy Town on the Thames near present Melbourne; and in the environs of Ohsweken on the south side of the Grand River. Four short articles have been published about the first group: Jasper Hill ("Big White Owl"), born at Moraviantown, remembered "My People the Delawares" [68]; Fred Bruemmer wrote "The Delawares of Moraviantown" [17]; and Frederick Coyne Hamil is the author of "Fairfield on the River Thames" [52] and "The Moravians of the River Thames" [53]. Arthur D. Graeff gives a general historical background of these Delaware groups in "Transplants of Pennsylvania Indian Nations in Ontario" [50].

The second group of Canadian Delaware descendants living at Muncy Town on the Thames have been incidentally mentioned in the literature, but no separate articles have been written about them. Someone should fill this void in the Delaware literature while information can still be obtained from elderly informants at Muncy Town.

*The Valley of the Six Nations*, edited by Charles M. Johnston [88], consists of a collection of documents about the Indian reservation on the Grand River, with many references to the third group of Delawares. Regrettably, the Delaware data are not in a separate section but are scattered throughout the text.

Harrington's "Vestiges of Material Culture among the Canadian Delawares" [56] illustrates domestic utensils and ceremonial specimens he collected in 1907 and gives comments about his visit. Frank G. Speck and his collaborator Jesse Moses, of Delaware descent, in *The Celestial Bear Comes down to Earth* [159], describe in detail a bear-sacrifice ceremony once practiced by the Delawares on the Grand River. Not only did bear grease, flesh, and pelts have a place in the native economic system, but Anthony F. C. Wallace illustrates how the relationship to the bear was institutionalized, in his "The Role of the Bear in Delaware Society" [186].

Returning to the main body of the tribe, the major study of the Delaware sojourn in Indiana is treated in an unpublished dissertation by Roger James Ferguson, "The White River Indiana Delawares: An Ethnohistoric Synthesis, 1795–1867" [40]. Ferguson made liberal use of Charles N. Thompson's *Sons of the Wilderness: John and William Conner* [167], which despite a misleading title, is an authentic account of the Delawares in Indiana and their role in the War of 1812. Thompson, however, made an error that Ferguson and others perpetuated. He mistakenly identified Mekinges (mother of the Delaware chiefs John and James Conner) as the daughter of Chief William Anderson. Weslager, *The Delaware Indian Westward Migration* [218], introduces evidence that she was a member of the Ketchum family. Ferguson made good use of the two volumes of *Governor's Messages and Letters: Messages and Letters of William Henry Harrison*, edited by Logan Esarey [38], especially Harrison's letters having to do with the Delawares during the War of 1812.

*Letter Book of the Indian Agency at Fort Wayne 1809– 1815*, edited by Gayle Thornbrough [169], contains letters about the Delawares written by two United States Indian agents, Benjamin F. Stickney and John Johnston. Johnston supervised the Delawares for many years and was well regarded by the tribe. Johnston's *Account of the Present State of the Indian Tribes Inhabiting Ohio* [89] gives population data and other information as of 17 June 1819. Further information about Johnston's contact with the Delawares is found in Leonard U. Hill, *John Johnston and the Indians in the Land of the Three Miamis* [69].

Jedidiah Morse, *Report to the Secretary of War of the United States on Indian Affairs* [119]; John Candee Dean, "Journal of Thomas Dean: A Voyage to Indiana in 1817" [26]; Charles Beatty, *The Journal of a Two Month's Tour with a View of Promoting Religion among the Frontier*

*Inhabitants of Pennsylvania* [7 ]; and Paul Weer, "Thomas Dean and the Delaware Towns" [195], are all reliable and extremely valuable descriptions of Delaware village locations, customs, and the names of their leaders during the period when the main body occupied Indiana.

When White settlers overran Indiana, the United States government moved the Delawares across the Mississippi to new homes in Missouri Territory. Eight years later the government moved them from Missouri to Kansas Territory, and in 1867 the Delawares finally migrated to Indian Territory, now Oklahoma. Weslager discusses these movements in *The Delaware Indians: A History* [213 ] and amplifies the details in *The Delaware Indian Westward Migration* [218 ].

Treaties with the United States provided for the cession of the Delawares' lands, and drawings of lands reserved for their use are reproduced in Charles C. Royce, *Indian Land Cession in the United States: The Eighteenth Annual Report of the Bureau of American Ethnology, 1896 – 1897* [145 ]. Royce undertook this project with infinite patience, and the work stands as a memorial to his persistence and skill.

The tragic story of the expatriation of the Delawares and other tribes is related by Grant Foreman in *The Last Trek of the Indians* [43]. Richard C. Adams emphasizes the mistreatment of his people in *A Delaware Indian Legend and the Story of Their Troubles* [1], a work he printed at his own expense in a futile effort to arouse White sympathy for the tribe.

No historical study has been written about the Delawares during the eight years they lived in Missouri, another gap that needs to be filled. John Treat Irving, Jr., was present when Delaware warriors from Missouri made peace with their Pawnee enemies in 1833, and he describes the appearance and dress of the Delaware chiefs in *Indian Sketches Taken during an Expedition to the Pawnee Tribes,* edited by John Francis McDermott [80, pp. 242–47]. Irving's account is just enough to whet the reader's interest, then he moves on to another subject!

A number of items have been published for the period when the Delawares lived in Kansas. Lewis Henry Morgan, *The Indian Journals, 1859–1862,* edited by Leslie A. White [118], contains a firsthand account of Morgan's discussions with Indian informants about clans, dances, chiefs, family names, and so on (pp. 51–54). Clara Gowing, a teacher in the Delaware Indian School, recorded her experiences in "Life among the Delaware Indians" [49], an account of particular interest because it is written from the point of view of a woman who came from the East to teach the Indian children.

"Two Minute Books of the Kansas Mission in the Forties," [174], provides the names of Delawares who became Christians. Alan W. Farley is the author of a popular account, "The Delaware Indians in Kansas 1829–1867" [39], which is inadequately documented but nevertheless is reasonably accurate.

A small group of Munsie-Delawares who remained in Kansas when the main body moved to Oklahoma

Reverend Joseph Romig, wrote about them in "The Chippewa and Munsee (or Christian) Indians of Franklin County, Kansas" [144]. Weslager wrote about the same group in "Enrollment List of Chippewa and Delaware-Munsies Living in Franklin County, Kansas, May 31, 1900" [216]. In this list of surviving Munsies he mistakenly gives the family name Supernaw as Supernan owing to a misinterpretation of the manuscript.

After the main body arrived in Oklahoma, where their descendants are still living, a number of publications were added to the literature. Muriel Wright includes ten pages on the Delawares in *A Guide to the Indian Tribes of Oklahoma* [222]. It is regrettable that space did not allow a more detailed account, but the author overtaxed the capacity of a single volume by attempting to discuss sixty-seven tribes.

Carolyn Thomas Foreman adds new information about one of the most famous Delaware war captains in "Black Beaver" [42]. Harry M. Roark's volume about the last Oklahoma Delaware chief, *Charles Journeycake: Indian Statesman and Christian Leader* [143], is more accurate than *The Indian Chief Journeycake*, a biased and often erroneous account written fifty years earlier by S. H. Mitchell [116]. Mitchell incorrectly stated that Journeycake became the principal chief in 1861. James Mooney, "The Passing of the Delaware Nation" [117], and Newcomb, "A Note on Cherokee-Delaware Pan Indianism" [125], both deal with the later period of Delaware history.

## Subdivisions and Clans

David Zeisberger stated in his "History of the Northern American Indians," edited by Archer Butler Hulbert and William Nathaniel Schwarze [223], that the Delawares were divided into three tribes: "Unamis, Wunalachticos, and Monsys." Later, John Heckewelder, in *History, Manners and Customs of the Indian Nations Who Once Inhabited Pennsylvania and Neighbouring States* [64], said that the Unami were known as the Turtle Tribe, the Unalachtigo (Wunalachticos) as the Turkey, and the Minsi, or Monseys, as the Wolf. The synonymity of these animal and tribal names has been widely quoted but is no longer acceptable to modern ethnohistorians.

As long ago as 1910, Mark R. Harrington, in "Some Customs of the Delaware Indians" [57], agreed that there were three tribal subdivisions, "Munsi, the Unami and the Unalachtigo," but said that it was incorrect to refer to them by animal names. He concluded that *each* of the subdivisions had a Turkey clan and a Wolf clan, and the Unami and Unalachtigo had Turtle clans, but this clan was lacking among the Munsi (p. 52). Harrington discussed the subject further in "A Preliminary Sketch of Lenape Culture" [58], after proving that the Oklahoma Delawares (Unami) were divided into three groupings: Wolf, Turtle, and Turkey.

The subject has been amplified in recent years by two authors who agree in principle with Harrington: "A Note on the Unalachtigo," by William A. Hunter [97, pp. 147–52], and "More about the Unalachtigo," by Weslager [217]. Related technical discussions of principal interest to linguists are Jay Miller, "Delaware Clan Names" [112], and Ives Goddard, "A Further Note on Delaware Clan Names" [48].

## Delaware Religion, Missions, and Missionaries

In *Religion and Ceremonies of the Lenape* [59], a highly recommended volume suitable for popular reading, Harrington made the first comprehensive study of Delaware religion. Speck's *A Study of the Delaware Indian Big House Ceremony* [152] is a technical account of the most important Delaware ceremony, rendered phonetically in the Delaware language with an English translation. Speck's data were obtained from a member of the Turkey group; if he had consulted a Wolf informant he would have found a different way of conducting the ceremony. Speck's *Oklahoma Delaware Ceremonies, Feasts and Dances* [155] treats of other ceremonies, and in this instance he obtained information from both Wolf and Turkey informants. Weslager, "The Delaware Indians, Their Gods, Their Religious Ceremonies" [206], summarized some of the data developed by Speck and Harrington in a brief popular account.

Horace L. McCracken, who was part Delaware, wrote a short paper, "The Delaware Big House" [109], based on information from other Delawares, since he never attended the ceremony. Richard C. Adams also obtained data from traditionalists for *The Ancient Religion of the Delaware Indians, and Observations and Reflections* [1].

James Howard, a professional anthropologist who lives in Oklahoma, augmented the earlier ceremonial accounts in "The Nanticoke-Delaware Skeleton Dance" [73]. Howard is also the author of *Ceremonial Dress of the Delaware Man* [74], illustrated with rare photographs of living and deceased Delawares in native costume. Tyrone Stewart has published "Oklahoma Delaware Woman's Dance Clothes" [163]; and bead and ribbon designs used in Delaware costumes are pictured by Gladys Tantaquidgeon in "Delaware Art Designs" [165]. She states that art motifs consist primarily of floral and geometric (angular) patterns, with human and animal figures very rare. Philhower's *The Art of the Lenape* is a brief and unimportant summation of costuming, tattooing, sculpturing, pottery-making, and so forth [134].

Reference has been made to early Swedish efforts to convert the Delawares. This was followed in 1743 by aggressive missionary work conducted by the Reverend David Brainerd, representing the Society for Propagating Christian Knowledge, as described by Jonathan Edwards in *Memoirs of the Rev. David Brainerd; Missionary to the Indians on the Borders of New York, New Jersey and Pennsylvania* [37]. The difficulties faced by a missionary appear throughout Brainerd's account, because the Delawares said that White Christians "lie, defraud, steal, and drink worse than the Indians" and that the influence of the English "made them quarrel and kill one another" (p. 342).

The activities of the Moravian church in attempting to convert the Delawares are discussed in detail by

Kenneth G. Hamilton, "Cultural Contributions of Moravian Missions among the Indians" [54]; William C. Reichel, editor, *Memorials of the Moravian Church*, volume 1 [141]; and George Henry Loskiel, *History of the Mission of the United Brethren among the Indians in North America* [102]. Throughout these accounts are specific comments about individual Delawares and Indian customs.

The most zealous Moravian missionary was David Zeisberger, who was adopted into the Delaware tribe. Valuable ethnohistorical notes can be obtained from "The Diaries of Zeisberger Relating to the First Missions in the Ohio Basin," edited by Hulbert and Schwarze [224], and *Diary of David Zeisberger, a Moravian Missionary among the Indians of Ohio,* edited by Eugene F. Bliss [10].

John Heckewelder was also an energetic missionary; see his *A Narrative of the Mission of the United Brethren among the Delaware and Mohegan Indians* [63 ]. Paul A. W. Wallace reconstructed the accounts of Heckewelder's association with the Delawares in "John Heckewelder's Indians and the Fenimore Cooper Tradition" [190 ], *Thirty Thousand Miles with John Heckewelder* [191 ], and "The John Heckewelder Papers" [192 ].

Elma E. Gray and her husband Leslie Robb Gray discuss the work of Moravian pastors in Canada as well as the United States in *Wilderness Christians: The Moravian Mission to the Delaware Indians* [51], a fully researched and well-documented volume. American readers may be surprised to learn that after the American army defeated the English in the Battle of Moraviantown during the War of 1812 they destroyed all the houses and churches of the converted Delawares.

While the Delawares lived in Indiana during an era of the revival of nativism, the Moravian missionaries suffered their worst reverses. This is treated in Abraham Luckenbach, *Biography of Brother Luckenbach, Written by Himself and Left for His Dear Children* [103], and in *The Moravian Mission on White River,* edited by Lawrence Henry Gipson [45]. Both volumes provide information about Delaware customs, names of chiefs of the three subdivisions, witchcraft, and notes on the social and economic deterioration of the tribe.

Isaac McCoy, *History of Baptist Indian Missions: Embracing Remarks on the Former and Present Condition of the Aboriginal Tribes* [108], is a story of the deterioration of the Delawares as seen through the eyes of a Baptist missionary.

After the Delawares reached Kansas, there was a rebirth of Christianity among them and a diminution in the practice of native religion, although the traditionalists resisted conversion. After they moved to Oklahoma a new cult came into existence, Peyotism, which was neither native Delaware nor Christian. This is discussed by Vincenzo M. Petrullo, *The Diabolic Root: A Study of Peyotism, the New Indian Religion among the Delawares* [132], and Newcomb, "The Peyote Cult of the Delaware Indians" [126]. Anthony F. C. Wallace, "New Religions among the Delaware Indians 1600–1900" [189] is also a relevant paper.

## The Delaware Language

Today the Delaware language is spoken fluently only by a few of the older people. The Canadian groups speak the Munsie dialect, which is so different from the Unami dialect spoken in Oklahoma that a Canadian Delaware and an Oklahoma Delaware cannot converse without practice, according to Ives Goddard in "The Delaware Language, Past and Present," [97, pp. 103–10]. Differences between the two dialects were discussed by John Dyneley Prince, "Notes on the Modern Minsi-Delaware Dialect" [138], and Charles F. Voegelin, "The Lenape and Munsee Dialects of Delaware, an Algonquian Language" [177]. A detailed discussion of the Delaware language was published by Voegelin, "Delaware an Eastern Algonquian Language" [179], and in another paper he gives examples of songs in the Delaware language sung during the Big House Ceremony, "Word Distortions in Delaware Big House and Walam Olum Songs" [178].

Two Delaware dictionaries have been published: *Zeisberger's Indian Dictionary*, edited by Eben Norton Horsford [72], gives German, English, Onondaga, and Delaware word equivalents. *A Lenape-English Dictionary* was edited by Daniel G. Brinton and the Reverend Albert Seqaqkind Anthony [16]. Anthony, who lived in Canada, spoke nothing but the Indian tongue until his thirteenth year; see Brinton's "Lenape Conversations" [15]. Actually the dictionary is a composite of words from the Munsie and Unami dialects, collected by at least five Moravian preachers over a hundred-year period; see Weslager, "A New Look at Brinton's Lenape-English Dictionary" [214]. Brinton also gives a Delaware word list with English translations in the *Lenape and Their Legends* [14, pp. 233–62], taken from Rafinesque's translation of the Walam Olum.

In 1785 Ebenezer Denny compiled a "Vocabulary of Words in Use with the Delaware and Shawnee Indians" [28], but most words are trader's jargon first discussed by John Dyneley Prince in "An Ancient New Jersey Indian Jargon" [139]. Goddard, in "The Ethnohistorical Implication of Early Delaware Linguistic Materials" [46], maintains that this jargon or pidginized form of the Delaware dialect was first used by the Dutch and then picked up by the Swedes and English, who thought they were learning the real Indian language.

Technical discussions of certain Delaware Indian words and phrases have been written by Goddard, "Delaware Kinship Terminology (with Comparative Notes)" [47], and Jay Miller, in "Delaware Alternative Classifications" [114] and "Delaware Anatomy: With Linguistic, Social and Medical Aspects" [115]. Dunlap adds further sources of Delaware linguistic data in "A Bibliographical Discussion of the Indian Languages of the Delmarva Peninsula" [33].

August C. Mahr is the author of a number of linguistic studies, including "Aboriginal Culture Traits as Reflected in Eighteenth Century Delaware Indian Tree Names" [105] and "Eighteenth Century Terminology of Delaware Indian Cultivation and Use of

Maize: A Semantic Analysis" [106]. Like the papers by Goddard and Miller, Mahr's accounts are highly technical and intended for scholars.

## Specialized Studies

Weslager, in "Name-Giving among the Delaware Indians" [212], deriving his information from both historical sources and a living name-giver, explains that each Delaware bore one real name (no surnames were used). This was supplemented by Weslager and James A. Rementer in "American Indian Genealogy and a List of Names Bestowed by a Delaware Indian Name-Giver" [219]. The name-giver cited in both articles was Touching Leaves (Mrs. Nora Thompson Dean), a fluent Delaware-speaker. The latter article enumerates thirty-four personal names she has bestowed and explains their meanings.

*Folk Medicine of the Delawares and Related American Indians*, by Gladys Tantaquidgeon [166], a Mohegan descendant, contains information obtained from James Webber, an Oklahoma Delaware, during his visit to Philadelphia in 1928. Webber's mother was a Munsie and his father was part Cherokee, which tends to detract from the data as being wholly Delaware. Weslager's *Magic Medicines of the Indians* [215] contains herb cures obtained from Touching Leaves, a full-blooded Delaware practitioner. George A. Hill also consulted Touching Leaves and three other Delaware informants in preparing a list of herb cures for "Delaware Ethnobotany" [67].

In "Lenape Basketry in Delaware," Arthur G. Volkman  [182 ] illustrates two baskets made by an aged
Delaware, "Indian Hannah," who died in 1802 in the
Chester County, Pennsylvania, poorhouse, the last full
blood who lived on the Brandywine. Volkman introduces evidence in his paper, "Chief Naaman—Naaman
Creek"  [181 ], that Chief Naaman, a Delaware-speaker
cited in 1654 Swedish records, had nothing to do with
Naaman's Creek in Delaware. There have been many
unsupported statements that the creek was named for
the chief.

Some popular writers are tempted to exaggerate
the role of certain Indian chiefs. Tamany (or
Tamenend) has almost been deified; at least he was
canonized in almanacs and referred to after his death
as Saint Tamany. Tamany was one of a number of
Delaware village or band chiefs, not a head chief over
all the Delaware, because that position did not exist in
the seventeenth century. Most of the articles about
Tamany have no basis in fact, and with one exception
they have been omitted from this bibliography. Local
tradition in New Britain Township, Bucks County,
Pennsylvania, has it that the aged Tamany was buried
near a spring on the right bank of Neshaminy Creek
after self-immolation; see "The Grave of Tamenend," by
Henry C. Mercer  [111 ]. Mercer's article springs from
"Tamany lore," not from archeological proof.

Tamany's grave is also reported to have been found
near Bush's Glen Creek in Wayne County, Pennsylvania, south of "Saint Tammany Flats"; see Max

Schrabish, *Archaeology of the Delaware River Valley* [147, pp. 45-46]. Schrabish says this has never been archeologically verified, although the tale persists. The facts are that there is no historical record of when Tamany died or where he was buried.

Specialized studies also include Speck's "The Grasshopper War in Pennsylvania, an Indian Myth That Become History" [156] and John Witthoft, "The Grasshopper War in Lenape Land" [220]. As recorded by Speck, the myth was a tale of how Delaware and Tuscarora children began to fight over possession of a grasshopper they were playing with. Soon their mothers and other adults became involved in the quarrel. Finally open war broke out between the two tribes. Witthoft's information led him to suggest that according to tradition the Grasshopper War was between the Delawares and the Shawnees, not the Tuscaroras. Since there is not even a hint in either written accounts or Indian tradition that the Delawares were ever at war in Pennsylvania with either the Shawnees or the Tuscaroras, these are obviously exaggerated folktales. Speck called them "an example of the type of Algonkian moral teaching with which the ethnologist has long been familiar" [156, p. 34].

Another folkloristic account—and this is of Delaware origin—tells that a catastrophic earthquake was sent by the Creator when the Delawares lived in Pennsylvania. This temblor, as reported by Speck in "The Great Pennsylvania Earthquake of Indian Days" [157], was apparently sent to punish them because of the indifference they they were showing to their religious duties. This terrifying experience is supposed to have resulted in a revival of native religion, and the Delawares were faithful thereafter in observing their tribal ceremonies. Speck points out that severe earth shocks have been recorded in Philadelphia, the earliest in October 1728, and it is reasonable to believe that the Delawares had experienced them long before.

In two brief personal accounts, "A Day in the Jersey Woods with a Delaware Indian" [153] and "Cruising the Eastern Woods with a Delaware Chief" [160], Speck shares with the reader the emotions of his Indian companion, Witapanoxwe ("Walks with Daylight"), on a canoe trip. The articles were practically duplications of each other. Although there are references to birds, herbs, and animals and to the Delaware's attitude toward them, one wishes that Speck had taken more time in the woods with the Indian and written a lengthier account of Witapanoxwe's rapport with the manifestations of nature.

The following brief comments about archeological references are included for readers interested in the subject, but it must be realized that the bibliography of books and papers dealing with the prehistoric excavations in New York, Pennsylvania, Delaware, and New Jersey is very extensive. Each of these four states has a state archeological society whose publications should be consulted for discussions of archeological periods and artifacts associated with its territory.

Some archeologists seem determined to relate pre-historic cultures to historical tribes, a practice that is invalid and results in questionable interpretations. E. W. Hawkes and Ralph Linton published *A Pre-Lenape Site in New Jersey* [62] after their excavation in 1915 of a site in southern New Jersey on a branch of Rancocas Creek between Masonville and Medford. All the artifacts uncovered were prehistoric, and there was no historical or artifactual evidence that it was occupied historically by Delaware Indians. Mary Butler also reported her archeological excavations conducted at "Two Lenape Rock Shelters near Philadelphia" [21]. How can one be certain that the historical tribal name "Lenape" is correctly applied to the prehistoric occupants of these and other precontact sites?

In *Delaware's Buried Past*, Weslager [198] discusses archeological findings in Delaware in a book intended for the general reader but refrains from associating prehistoric artifacts with the historical Delawares. Dorothy Cross, in *Archaeology of New Jersey* [24], avoids the error of identifying her archeological discoveries with historical Delaware Indians, and John Witthoft exercises similar restraint in *Indian Prehistory of Pennsylvania* [221].

Glenn A. Black, "An Archaeological Consideration of the Walam Olum" [184, pp. 292–348], clearly explains the inconsistency of endeavoring to identify a basic prehistoric culture complex as being specifically Lenape. Black properly insists this can be done only if a site can be identified incontrovertibly as being occupied by the Lenape in historic times through historical documentation and the uncovering of objects of White man's manufacture traded with the Indians. Kraft, in "Indian Prehistory of New Jersey" [97, pp. 1–55 ], recognizes the difference between reconstructing prehistory and identifying historic contact period sites, which are infrequent in New Jersey. In fact, he points out that European trade items are very scarce at New Jersey sites.

According to Aleš Hrdlička, *Physical Anthropology of the Lenape or Delawares and of Eastern Indians in General* [75 ],   the skeletal remains of the Lenape exhibit certain anatomical characteristics that he illustrates and discusses in technical language. Actually, Hrdlička's study was limited to the remains of approximately fifty seven skeletons uncovered in 1914 by George G. Heye and George H. Pepper on Minisink Island, as reported in *Exploration of a Munsee Cemetery near Montague, New Jersey* [66 ].   An adjacent area was excavated in 1947 by William A. Ritchie and described in *The Bell-Philhower Site, Sussex County, New Jersey*  [142 ]. As Kraft states in *The Minisink Settlements*  [98, p.2 ], a clear distinction must be made between the Delawares and the Minisinks or Munsies, which has been pointed out earlier in this essay. Thus, Hrdlička's analysis applies to the physical anthropology of the Minisinks and not necessarily to the Delawares in general. Although thousands of artifacts, skeletal remains, and many examples of pottery vessels have been uncovered on prehistoric sites south of the Delaware

Water Gap on both sides of the Delaware River, cultural and anatomical data are still lacking, as Black fully recognized, to relate this material to the historical Delaware Indians.

One should also be aware that Charles Beatty, who visited the migrant Delawares when they were living in Ohio in 1766, says in *The Journal of a Two Month's Tour* [7] that, according to a chronological record the Delawares kept with wampum beads, the tribe first came to the Delaware River basin 370 years earlier. If credence can be given to this information, as Eli Lilly stated in "Speculations on the Chronology of the Walam Olum and Migration of the Lenape" [184, pp. 273–85], they were latecomers to the East and did not arrive there until A.D. 1396. This too remains inconclusive.

## ALPHABETICAL LIST AND INDEX

*Denotes items suitable for secondary school students

Item
no.

Essay
page
no.

[1]  *  Adams, Richard C. 1899. *A Delaware Indian Legend and the Story of Their Troubles.* Washington, D.C.                                    (31, 35)

[2]  *  ———. 1904. *The Ancient Religion of the Delaware Indians and Observations and Reflections.* Washington, D.C.: The Law Reporter Printing Co. (Contains oration made in Big House Ceremony, Nov. 1903 by the Delaware chief "Colonel Jackson," pp. 28-29.)

[3]     ———. 1906. "A Brief History of the Delaware Indians." *Senate Document No. 501, 59th Congress, 1st session,* pp. 1-70. Washington: Government Printing Office.                                         (3)

[4]     Allinson, Samuel. 1875. "Fragmentary History of the New Jersey Indians." *Proceedings of the New Jersey Historical Society,* 2nd series, vol. 4, no. 1. (Contains data on Delaware-Brotherton reservation in New Jersey.)                            (22)

[5]     Aupaumut, Hendrick. 1827. "A Narrative of an Embassy to the Western In-

dians [1792]." *Memoirs of the Historical Society of Pennsylvania* 2, part 1, pp. 61-131. (27)

[6] Barnes, Carol. 1968. "Subsistence and Social Organization of the Delaware Indians: 1600 A.D." *Bulletin of the Philadelphia Anthropological Society* 20, no. 1, pp. 15-29. (15)

[7] Beatty, Charles. 1768. *The Journal of a Two Month's Tour With a View of Promoting Religion Among the Frontier Inhabitants of Pennsylvania.* London: William Davenhill. (Reprinted 1962 in *Journals of Charles Beatty 1762–1769,* ed. Guy S. Klett. University Park: Pennsylvania State College Press.) (31, 47)

[8] Becker, Marshall J. 1976. "The Okehocking: A Remnant Band of Delaware Indians." *Pennsylvania Archaeologist* 46, no. 3, pp. 24-61. (12)

[9] * Bleeker, Sonia. 1953. *The Delaware Indians.* New York: William Morrow & Company. (15)

[10] Bliss, Eugene F., ed. and trans. 1885. *Diary of David Zeisberger, a Moravian Missionary Among the Indians of Ohio [1781–1798],* 2 vols. Cincinnati: Robert Clarke and Co. for the Historical and Philosophical Society of Ohio. (37)

[11]    Bond, Beverley W., Jr., ed. 1926. "The Captivity of Charles Stuart, 1755–1757." *Mississippi Valley Historical Review* 13: 58-81.    (26)

[12]    Boyd, Julian P. ed. 1938. *Indian Treaties Printed by Benjamin Franklin, 1736–1762.* Philadelphia: Historical Society of Pennsylvania.    (20)

[13] *  Brickell, John. 1842. "Narrative of John Brickell's Captivity among the Delaware Indians." *The American Pioneer* 1: 43-56. Cincinnati: John S. Williams.    (26)

[14]    Brinton, Daniel G. 1885. *The Lenape and their Legends with the Complete Text and Symbols of the Walam Olum.* Library of Aboriginal American Literature, Number 5. Philadelphia: D. G. Brinton. (Reissued 1976 by AMS Press, Inc., New York:)    (6, 40)

[15] *  _____. 1888. "Lenape Conversations." *Journal of American Folklore,* vol. 1, no. 1, pp. 37-43.    (39)

[16]    _____ and Albert Seqaqkind Anthony, eds. 1888. *A Lenape-English Dictionary.* Philadelphia: Historical Society of Pennsylvania. (Reissued by AMS Press, Inc., New York.)    (39)

[17] *  Bruemmer, Fred. 1964. "The Delawares

of Moraviantown." *Canadian Geographical Journal* 68: 95-97. (28)

[18] Brunner, D. B. 1881. *The Indians of Berks County, Pa., being a Summary of All the Tangible Records of the Aborigines of Berks County.* (2nd ed., 1897. Reading: Eagle Book Print.) (14)

[19] Buck, William J. 1883. "Lappawinzo and Tishcohan, Chiefs of the Lenni Lenape." *Pennsylvania Magazine of History and Biography* 7:215-218. (Reprinted in *Bulletin of the Archaeological Society of New Jersey,* Spring-Summer, 1974, pp. 26-28.) (9)

[20] Bushnell, David I., Jr. 1916. "The Virginia Frontier in History, 1778." *Virginia Magazine of History and Biography* 24:168-179. (Contains contemporary account of treaties with Delawares at Pittsburgh and Logstown.) (28)

[21] Butler, Mary. 1947. "Two Lenape Rock Shelters Near Philadelphia." *American Antiquity* 12:246-255. (45)

[22] Campanius, Johannes. 1696. *Lutheri Catechismus, etc.* Stockholm: Burchardi. (Facsimile edition entitled *Martin Luther's Little Catechism; Translated into Algonquian Indian by Johannes Campanius,*

1937, for the celebration of the New Sweden Tercentenary Jubilee. Stockholm and Uppsala: Ivar Haeggstrom and Almqvist & Wiksell.)    (11)

[23] * Carter, Jane Levis. 1976. *The Down River People of the Lenni-Lenape Indians.* A special extraction of Delaware Indian material from *Edgmont, the Story of a Township* by Jane Levis Carter, Kennett Square, Penna: KNA Press, Inc.    (14)

[24] Cross, Dorothy. 1941. *Archaeology of New Jersey* 1. Trenton: Archaeological Society of New Jersey and New Jersey State Museum.    (45)

[25] * ———. 1965. *New Jersey's Indians.* Report No. 1, New Jersey State Museum, Trenton.    (19)

[26] Dean, John Candee. 1918. "Journal of Thomas Dean, a Voyage to Indiana in 1817." *Indiana Historical Collections* 6, no. 2, pp. 273-345. Indianapolis: Indiana Historical Bureau.    (30)

[27] Deardorff, Merle H. 1946. "Zeisberger's Allegheny River Indian Towns: 1767–1770." *Pennsylvania Archaeologist* 16:2-19.    (25)

[28] Denny, Ebenezer. 1860. "Vocabulary of Words in Use with the Delaware and

Shawanee Indians [1785]." *Memoirs of the Historical Society of Pennsylvania* 7:478-485. (40)

[29] de Valinger, Leon, Jr. 1941. *Indian Land Sales in Delaware.* Wilmington: Archaeological Society of Delaware (Contains addendum, pp. 14-24: C. A. Weslager, "A Discussion of the Family Hunting Territory Question in Delaware.) (20)

[30] De Vries, David Pietersz. 1857. "Voyages from Holland to America, A.D. 1632 to 1644." Trans. Henry C. Murphy. *Collections of the New-York Historical Society,* second series, vol. 3, pp. 1-136. (English version of *Korte Historiael ende Journeels Aenteyekeninge,* 's-Gravenhage, 1655.) (11)

[31] * Donehoo, George P. 1928. *A History of the Indian Villages and Place Names in Pennsylvania with Numerous Historical Notes and References.* Harrisburg: The Telegraph Press. (25)

[32] Downes, Randolph C. 1940. *Council Fires on the Upper Ohio.* Pittsburgh: University of Pittsburgh Press. (27)

[33] Dunlap, Arthur R. 1949. "A Bibliographical Discussion of the Indian Languages of the Delmarva Peninsula." *Bul-*

*letin of the Archaeological Society of Delaware*
4, no. 5, pp. 2-5.                                        (40)

[34]   Dunlap, A. R., and C. A. Weslager. 1967.
"More Missing Evidence: Two Depositions by Early Swedish Settlers." *Pennsylvania Magazine of History and Biography*
91:35-45.                                                (12)

[35]   _____. 1967. "Two Delaware Valley Indian Place-Names (*Queonemysing* and
*Mageckqueshou*)." *Names* 15:197-202.      (8)

[36]   Du Ponceau, Peter S., and J. Francis
Fisher. 1836. "A Memoir on the His-
tory of the Celebrated Treaty Made by
William Penn with the Indians Under
the Elm Tree at Shackamaxon in the
Year 1682." *Memoirs of the Historical
Society of Pennsylvania* 3, part 2, pp.
145-203.                                                 (21)

[37]   Edwards, Jonathan. 1822. *Memoirs of the
Rev. David Brainerd; Missionary to the Indians on the Borders of New York, New Jersey and Pennsylvania.* Ed. Sereno Edwards Dwight. New Haven: S. Con-
verse.                                                    (36)

[38]   Esarey, Logan, ed. 1922. *Governor's
Messages and Letters. Messages and Letters
of William Henry Harrison,* 2 vols. *Indi-*

*ana Historical Collections* 7, 9. Indianapolis. (30)

[39] * Farley, Alan W. 1955. "The Delaware
Indians in Kansas 1829–1867." *The
Trail Guide,* 1, no. 1, pp. 7-22. (32)

[40] Ferguson, Roger James. 1972. "The
White River Indiana Delawares: An
Ethnohistoric Synthesis, 1795–1867."
Ed. D. Dissertation, Ball State Univer-
sity, Muncie, Indiana. (29)

[41] Flannery, Regina. 1939. *An Analysis of
Coastal Algonquian Culture. The Catholic
University of America Anthropological
Series* 7. Washington, D.C. (Reissued by
AMS Press, Inc.) (16)

[42] * Foreman, Carolyn Thomas. 1946.
"Black Beaver." *The Chronicles of Oklahoma* 24:269-292. (33)

[43] * Foreman, Grant. 1946. *The Last Trek of
the Indians.* Chicago: University of
Chicago Press. (31)

[44] Gehring, Charles T., ed. 1977. *New
York Historical Manuscripts: Dutch Vols.
20-21, Delaware Papers* [1644–1682].
Baltimore: Genealogical Publishing Co. (17)

[45] Gipson, Lawrence Henry ed. 1938. *The
Moravian Mission on White River* [In-

diana]. *Indiana Historical Collections* 23.
Indianapolis.    Indiana    Historical
Bureau.    (38)

[46]    Goddard, Ives. 1971. "The Ethnohistorical Implications of Early Delaware
Linguistics Materials." *Man in the Northeast* 1:14-26.    (40)

[47]    _____. 1973. "Delaware Kinship
Terminology (with Comparative
Notes)." *Studies in Linguistics* 23:39-56.    (40)

[48]    _____. 1974. "A Further Note on Delaware Clan Names." *Man in the Northeast* 7:106-109.    (35)

[49] * Gowing, Clara. 1912. "Life Among the
Delaware Indians [1859–1864]." *Collections of the Kansas State Historical Society*
12:183-193.    (32)

[50] * Graeff, Arthur D. 1948. "Transplants
of Pennsylvania Indian Nations in Ontario." *Pennsylvania History* 15:180-193.    (28)

[51]    Gray, Elma E., in collaboration with
Leslie Robb Gray. 1956. *Wilderness
Christians, the Moravian Mission to the De-
laware Indians*. Toronto: The Macmillan
Company of Canada, Limited.    (37)

[52] * Hamil, Frederick Coyne. 1939. "Fair-
child on the River Thames." *Ohio State*

*Archaeological and Historical Quarterly* 48:1-19. (28)

[53] * ———. 1949. "The Moravians of the River Thames." *Michigan History* 33:97-116: Lansing: Michigan Historical Commission. (28)

[54] Hamilton, Kenneth G. 1951. "Cultural Contributions of Moravian Missions Among the Indians." *Pennsylvania History* 18:1-15. (37)

[55] Hanna, Charles A. 1911. *The Wilderness Trail.* 2 vols. New York and London: G.P. Putnam's Sons. (Reprinted by AMS Press, Inc.) (23)

[56] Harrington, Mark R. 1908. "Vestiges of Material Culture Among the Canadian Delawares." *American Anthropologist*, n.s., 10:408-418. (29)

[57] * ———. "Some Customs of the Delaware Indians." *Museum Journal*, vol. 1, no. 3, pp. 52-60, Philadelphia: University of Pennsylvania. (34)

[58] ———. 1913. "A Preliminary Sketch of Lenape Culture." *American Anthropologist*, n.s., 15:208-235. (34)

[59] ———. 1921. *Religion and Ceremonies of the Lenape. Museum of the American Indi-*

an, *Heye Foundation, Indian Notes and Monographs* 19. New York. (Reprinted by AMS Press, Inc.)                    (35)

[60] * _____. 1933. "The Life of a Lenape Boy." *Pennsylvania Archaeologist* 3, no. 4, pp. 3-8.                                   (14)

[61] * _____. 1938. *Dickon Among the Indians.* Chicago, Philadelphia: The John C. Winston Company. (Reprinted 1963 as *The Indians of New Jersey, Dickon Among the Lenapes.* New Brunswick, N.J.: Rutgers University Press.)                    (5)

[62]   Hawkes, E.W., and Ralph Linton. 1916. *A Pre-Lenape Site in New Jersey. University Museum Anthropological Publications* 6, no. 3. Philadelphia: University of Pennsylvania Museum.                        (45)

[63]   Heckewelder, John. 1820. *A Narrative of the Mission of the United Brethren Among the Delaware and Mohegan Indians.* Philadelphia: McCarty and Davis. (Reprinted by Arno Press.)                (37)

[64]   _____. 1819. *An Account of the History, Manners, and Customs, of the Indian Nations Who Once Inhabited Pennsylvania and the Neighbouring States. Transactions of the Historical and Literary Committee of the American Philosophical Society* 1.

Philadelphia. (Rev. ed. 1876, ed. William C. Reichel. *Memoirs of the Historical Society of Pennsylvania* 12. Philadelphia.)(23, 34)

[65]    Herman, Mary W. 1950. "A Reconstruction of Aboriginal Delaware Culture from Contemporary Sources." *Kroeber Anthropology Society Papers* 1:45-77. Berkeley.                  (20)

[66]    Heye, George G., and George H. Pepper. 1915. *Exploration of a Munsee Cemetery Near Montague, New Jersey. Contributions from the Museum of the American Indian, Heye Foundation* 2, no. 1. New York. (Reprinted by AMS Press, Inc.)    (46)

[67]    Hill, George A. 1971. "Delaware Ethnobotany." *Oklahoma Anthropological Society Newsletter* 19, no. 3. pp. 3-18.    (41)

[68]  * Hill, Jasper ("Big White Owl"). 1943. "My People, the Delawares." *Bulletin of the Archaeological Society of Delaware* 4:9-13.                  (28)

[69]    Hill, Leonard U. 1957. *John Johnston and the Indians in the Land of the Three Miamis.* Piqua, Ohio, printed Columbus, Ohio: Stoneman Press.    (30)

[70]    Hodge, Frederick Webb, ed. 1907-1910. *Handbook of American Indians*

*North of Mexico. Bureau of American Ethnology Bulletin* 30. 2 vols. Washington, D.C.: Government Printing Office.    (3)

[71]    Holm, Thomas Campanius. 1834. "A Short Description of the Province of New Sweden. Now called by the English Pennsylvania in America [1702]." Trans. Peter S. Du Ponceau. *Memoirs of the Historical Society of Pennsylvania* 3, part 1, pp. 1-166.    (10)

[72]    Horsford, Eben Norton, ed. 1887. *Zeisberger's Indian Dictionary*. Cambridge: John Wilson and Son, University Press.    (39)

[73]    Howard, James H. 1975. "The Nanticoke-Delaware Skeleton Dance." *American Indian Quarterly* 2:1-13.    (36)

[74] *    _____. 1976. *Ceremonial Dress of the Delaware Man. Bulletin of the Archaeological Society of New Jersey* 33.    (36)

[75]    Hrdliška, Aleš.1916. *Physical Anthropology of the Lenape or Delawares and of the Eastern Indians in General. Bureau of American Ethnology Bulletin* 62; Washington: Government Printing Office. (Reprinted by AMS Press, Inc.)    (46)

[76] *    Hunter, William A. 1954. "The Ohio, the Indian's Land." *Pennsylvania History* 21:338-350.    (25)

[77] ———. 1954. "John Hays' Diary and Journal of 1760." *Pennsylvania Archaeologist* 24, no. 2, pp. 63-83. (25)

[78] * ———. 1956. "Victory at Kittanning." *Pennsylvania History* 23:376-407. (25)

[79] ———. 1960. *Forts on the Pennsylvania Frontier, 1753-1758.* Harrisburg: The Pennsylvania Historical and Museum Commission. (25)

[80] Irving, John Treat, Jr. 1955. *Indian Sketches Taken During an Expedition to the Pawnee Tribes.* Ed. John Francis McDermott. Norman: University of Oklahoma Press. (32)

[81] Jennings, Francis P. 1963. "A Vanishing Indian: Francis Parkman Versus His Sources." *Pennsylvania Magazine of History and Biography* 87:306-323. (26)

[82] ———. 1965. "The Delaware Interregnum." *Pennsylvania Magazine of History and Biography* 89:174-198. (21)

[83] ———. 1968. "Incident at Tulpehocken." *Pennsylvania History* 35:335-355. (21)

[84] ———. 1970. "The Scandalous Indian Policy of William Penn's Sons: Deeds and Documents of the Walking Purchase." *Pennsylvania History* 37:19-39. (21)

[85]    ———. 1971. "The Constitutional
        Evolution of the Covenant Chain."
        *Proceedings of the American Philosophical
        Society* 115:88-96.                          (24)

[86]    Johnson, Amandus. 1911. *The Swedish
        Settlements on the Delaware: Their History
        and Relation to the Indians, Dutch and
        English, 1638-1664.* 2 vols. Philadel-
        phia: University of Pennsylvania. (Re-
        printed 1969. Baltimore: Genealogical
        Publishing Co.)                              (18)

[87]    ———, editor and translator. 1930. *The
        Instruction for Johan Printz, Governor of
        New Sweden.* Philadelphia: The Swedish
        Colonial Society.                             (9)

[88]    Johnston, Charles M., ed. 1964. *The
        Valley of the Six Nations.* Toronto: The
        Champlain Society for the Government
        of Ontario, University of Toronto
        Press.                                       (29)

[89]    Johnston, John. 1820. *Account of the
        Present State of the Indian Tribes Inhabit-
        ing Ohio: Letter from John Johnston Agent
        of Indian Affairs at Piqua to Caleb Atwater
        Esq.* [June 17, 1819]. *Transactions of the
        American Antiquarian Society* 1:269-299.
        (Gives statistics on Delawares and other
        tribes).                                     (30)

[90] Jones, Rev. David. 1865. *A Journal of Two Visits Made to Some Nations of Indians on the West Side of the River Ohio, in the Years 1772 and 1773*. New York: Sabin Reprints. (Also reprinted by Arno Press). (27)

[91] Kappler, Charles J., ed. 1904-1941. *Indian Affairs: Laws and Treaties*. 5 vols. Washington, D.C.: Government Printing Office. (28)

[92] Kellogg, Louise P., ed. 1916. *Frontier Advance on the Upper Ohio 1778-1779. Publications of the State Historical Society of Wisconsin, Collections* 23, *Draper Series* 4, Madison. (27)

[93] _____. 1917. *Frontier Retreat on the Upper Ohio 1779-1781. Publications of the State Historical Society of Wisconsin, Collections* 24, *Draper Series* 5, Madison. (27)

[94] Kenny, James. 1913. "Journal of James Kenny, 1761-1763." Ed. John W. Jordan. *The Pennsylvania Magazine of History and Biography* 37:1-47, 152-201. (26)

[95] Keyser, Charles S. 1882. *Penn's Treaty with the Indians.* Philadelphia: D. McKay. (20)

[96] Kinietz, Vernon. 1946. *Delaware Culture Chronology. Indian Historical Society Pre-*

*history Research Series* 3, no. 1, Indianapolis (Reprinted by AMS Press, Inc.)    (4)

[97]    Kraft, Herbert C. 1974. *A Delaware Indian Symposium. Pennsylvania Historical and Museum Commission Anthropological Series* 4, Harrisburg. (Contains articles by Ives Goddard, William A. Hunter, Francis P. Jennings, Herbert C. Kraft, Melburn D. Thurman, C. A. Weslager, and Albright G. Zimmerman). (24, 34, 39, 46)

[98]    ————. 1977. *The Minisink Settlements: an Investigation into a Prehistoric and Early Historic Site in Sussex County, New Jersey.* South Orange. Archeological Research Center, Seton Hall University Museum.    (13, 46)

[99]    Laet, John [Joannes] de. 1841. "Extracts from the New World, or a Description of the West Indies [1625]." *Collections of the New-York Historical Society,* second series, 1:282-316.    (11)

[100] * Leslie, Vernon. 1973. *Faces in Clay.* Middletown, N.Y.: T. E. Henderson.    (13)

[101]    Lindeström, Peter. 1925. *Geographia Americae with an Account of the Delaware Indians.* Ed. and trans. Amandus Johnson. Philadelphia: The Swedish Colonial Society.    (9, 13)

[102] Loskiel, George Henry. 1794. *History of the Mission of the United Brethren Among the Indians in North America.* Trans. Christian Ignatius La Trobe. London: Brethren's Society for the Furtherance of the Gospel. (37)

[103] Luckenbach, Abraham. 1917. "Biography of Brother Luckenbach, written by Himself and Left for his Dear Children." [c. 1850] Trans. Harry Emilius Stocker. In Stocker, *A History of the Moravian Mission Among the Indians on the White River in Indiana*, pp. 131-80, Bethlehem: Times Publishing Co. (38)

[104] MacLeod, William Christie. 1922. "The Family Hunting Territory and Lenape Political Organization." *American Anthropologist* 24:449-463. (20, 22)

[105] Mahr, August C. 1954. "Aboriginal Culture Traits As Reflected in Eighteenth Century Delaware Indian Tree Names." *Ohio Journal of Science* 54:380-387. (40)

[106] _____. 1955. "Eighteenth Century Terminology of Delaware Indian Cultivation and Use of Maize: a Semantic Analysis." *Ethnohistory* 2:209-40. (41)

[107] [Maryland]. 1883- . *Archives of Maryland.* Eds. William Hand Brown *et. al.* 72

vols. published to date. Baltimore: Maryland Historical Society.    (17)

[108]  McCoy, Isaac. 1840. *History of Baptist Indian Missions.* Washington: William M. Morrison. (New York: H. and S. Raynor; Utica: Bennett, Backus and Hawley.)    (38)

[109] * McCracken, H. L. 1956. "The Delaware Big House." *The Chronicles of Oklahoma* 34:183-192. Oklahoma City: Oklahoma Historical Society.    (35)

[110] * Mercer, Henry C. 1885. *The Lenape Stone or The Indian and the Mammoth.* New York and London: G. P. Putnam's Sons.    (4)

[111]  _____. 1893. "The Grave of Tamenend (Tammany)." *Magazine of American History* 29:255-261. [Reprinted in *Bucks County Historical Society Papers* 2 (1909): 58-66].    (42)

[112]  Miller, Jay. 1973. "Delaware Clan Names." *Man in the Northeast* 6:57-60.    (35)

[113]  _____. 1974. "The Delaware as Women: a Symbolic Solution." *American Ethnologist* 1:507-514.    (23)

[114]  _____. 1975. "Delaware Alternative Classifications." Anthropological Linguistics, 17, no. 9, pp. 434-444.    (40)

[115]    ———. 1977. "Delaware Anatomy: with Linguistic, Social, and Medical Aspects." *Anthropological Linguistics* 19, no. pp. 144-166.                    (40)

[116]    Mitchell, S. H. 1895. *The Indian Chief Journeycake*. Philadelphia: The American Baptist Publication Society.                    (33)

[117]    Mooney, James. 1911. "The Passing of the Delaware Nation." *Proceedings of the Mississippi Valley Historical Assoication*, 3 (1909-1910): 329-340.                    (33)

[118]    Morgan, Lewis Henry. 1959. *The Indian Journals, 1859-1862*. Ed. Leslie A. White. Ann Arbor: University of Michigan Press.                    (32)

[119]    Morse, Jedidiah. 1822. *A Report to the Secretary of War of the United States, on Indian Affairs*. New Haven: S. Converse.                    (30)

[120]    Myers, Albert Cook, ed. 1912. *Narratives of Early Pennsylvania, West New Jersey and Delaware 1630-1707*. New York: Charles Scribners Sons. (Contains references to Delaware Indians by David Pietersz. DeVries, Thomas Yong, Johan Printz, Johan Rising, William Penn, Gabriel Thomas, Francis Daniel Pastorius, and other seventeenth century observers.)                    (8, 22)

[121] * _____. 1937. *William Penn: His Own Account of the Lenni Lenape or Delaware Indians, 1783.* Moylan, Pa.: privately printed. (Reprinted 1977, Middle Atlantic Press, Wallingford, Penna.)    (8, 21)

[122] * Nelson, William. 1894. *The Indians of New Jersey, Their Origin and Development, Manners and Customs, Language, Religion and Government.* Paterson: The Press. (Includes Delaware Indian word list, "The Salem Interpreter").    (19)

[123]    _____. 1904. *Personal Names of Indians of New Jersey.* Paterson: The Paterson History Club.    (19)

[124]    Newcomb, William W., Jr. 1955. "The Walam Olum of the Delaware Indians in Perspective." *The Texas Journal of Science* 7:57-62. (Reprinted in *Bulletin of the Archaeological Society of New Jersey* 30 (1974) pp. 29-32).    (7)

[125]    _____. 1955. "A Note on Cherokee-Delaware Pan-Indianism." *American Anthropologist* 57:1041-1045.    (33)

[126]    _____. 1956. "The Peyote Cult of the Delaware Indians." *Texas Journal of Science* 8:202-211.    (38)

[127]    _____. 1956. *The Culture and Acculturation of the Delaware Indians. Museum of*

*Anthropology, University of Michigan, Anthropological Papers* 10. Ann Arbor. (4)

[128] [New-York Historical Society.] 1841. *Collections.* Second Series, 1. New York: Printed for the Society by H. Ludwig. (Contains accounts relating to the Delawares by Adriaen Van der Donck, David Pietersz de Vries, John de Laet, and other seventeenth century observers.) (17)

[129] O'Callaghan, Edmund B., ed. 1853-1887. *Documents Relative to the Colonial History of the State of New York*, 15 vols., Albany: Weed, Parsons and Co. (Vol. 12 dealing with the Delaware River Valley, 1624-1682, edited and translated by B. Fernow.) (17)

[130] [Pennsylvania]. 1838-1853. *Minutes of the Provincial Council of Pennsylvania from the Organization to the Termination of the Proprietary Government.* 16 vols. Vols. 11-16 titled *Minutes of the Supreme Executive Council of Pennsylvania.* Ed. Samuel Hazard. Harrisburg and Philadelphia. (Vols. 1-3 reprinted 1852 with different pagination.) (17)

[131] *Pennsylvania Archives.* 1852-1949. Ed. Samuel Hazard *et al.* 9 series, 138 vols. Philadelphia and Harrisburg. (16)

[132]    Petrullo, Vincenzo M. 1934. *The Diabolic Root: A Study of Peyotism, the New Indian Religion Among the Delawares.* Philadelphia: University of Pennsylvania Press. (Reprinted by Octagon Books, 1975.)    (38)

[133]    Philhower, Charles A. 1931. "Some Personal Characteristics of the Lenape Indians." *Proceedings of the New Jersey Historical Society* 16:138-161.    (15)

[134] * _____. 1932. *The Art of the Lenape.* Leaflet no. 1, The Archaeological Society of New Jersey, 4 pages.    (36)

[135] * _____. 1933. *The Human Face in Lenape Archaeology.* Leaflet no. 2, The Archaeological Society of New Jersey, 6 pages.    (5)

[136] * _____. 1936. "The Indians of the Morris County [New Jersey] Area." *Proceedings of the New Jersey Historical Society* 54:249-267.    (13)

[137]    _____. 1953-1954. "The Historic Minisink Site," *Bulletin of the Archaeological Society of New Jersey* 7 (1953):1-9; 8 (1954):1-7.    (13)

[138]    Prince, J. Dyneley. 1900. "Notes on the Modern Minsi-Delaware Dialect." *American Journal of Philology* 21:295-302.    (39)

[139] ———. 1912. "An Ancient New Jersey Indian Jargon." *American Anthropologist*, n.s., 14:508-524. (40)

[140] * Reed, Henry Clay, ed. 1947. *Delaware, A History of the First State*. 3 vols. New York: Lewis Historical Publishing Co. (3)

[141] Reichel, William C. ed. 1870. *Memorials of the Moravian Church*, vol. 1. Philadelphia: J.B. Lippincott and Co. (37)

[142] Ritchie, William A. 1949. *The Bell-Philhower Site, Sussex County, New Jersey. Indiana Historical Society Prehistory Research Series* 3. Indianapolis. (46)

[143] Roark, Harry M. 1970 [1948]. *Charles Journeycake: Indian Statesman and Christian Leader*. Published Th. D.Diss. Dallas: Taylor Publishing Co. (33)

[144] Romig, Rev Joseph. 1909-1910. "The Chippewa and Munsee (or Christian) Indians of Franklin County, Kansas." *Kansas State Historical Society Collections* 11:314-323. (33)

[145] Royce, Charles C. 1899. *Indian Land Cessions in the United States: Eighteenth Annual Report of the Bureau of American Ethnology, 1896-1897*. Part 2: Washington, D.C. Reprinted by Arno Press). (31)

[146]    Ruttenber, Edward M. 1872. *History of the Indian Tribes of Hudson's River.* Albany: J. Munsell. (Reissued 1971, Port Washington, N.Y.: Ira J. Friedman Division, Kennikat Press.)                    (18)

[147]    Schrabisch, Max. 1930. *Archaeology of Delaware River Valley. Publications of the Pennsylvania Historical Commission* 1. Harrisburg.                    (43)

[148]    Sipe, Chester Hale. 1927. *Indian Chiefs of Pennsylvania.* Butler, Pa: Ziegler Printing Co.                    (25)

[149]    _____. 1929. *The Indian Wars of Pennsylvania.* Harrisburg: The Telegraph Press.                    (25)

[150]    Skinner, Alanson B. 1915. *The Indians of Greater New York.* Cedar Rapids: Torch Press. (See "Customs of the Delaware," pp. 48-69.)                    (19)

[151]    _____. 1920. "Two Lenape Stone Masks from Pennsylvania and New Jersey." *Museum of the American Indian, Heye Foundation, Indian Notes and Monographs, Miscellaneous Series* 3. New York.                    (5)

[152]    Speck, Frank G. 1931 *A Study of the Delaware Indian Big House Ceremony. Publications of the Pennsylvania Historical Commission* 2, Harrisburg.                    (35)

[153] * _____. 1932. "A Day in the Jersey Woods with a Delaware Indian." *The General Magazine* 35:9-12, University of Virginia. (44)

[154] _____. 1935. "Speaking of the Delawares." *Pennsylvania Archaeologist* 4, no. 4, pp. 3-9. (14)

[155] _____. 1937. *Oklahoma Delaware Ceremonies, Feasts and Dances. Memoirs of the American Philosophical Society* 7. Philadelphia. (35)

[156] * _____. 1942. "The Grasshopper War in Pennsylvania, an Indian Myth That Became History," *Pennsylvania Archaeologist* 12:31-34. (43)

[157] _____. 1942. "The Great Pennsylvania Earthquake of Indian Days." *Pennsylvania Archaeologist* 12:57-59. (43)

[158] _____. 1943. "The Wapanachki Delawares and the English; Their Past as Viewed by an Ethnologist." *Pennsylvania Magazine of History and Biography* 67:319-344. (1)

[159] _____, in collaboration with Jesse Moses. 1945. *The Celestial Bear Comes Down to Earth. Scientific Publications* 7. Reading, Pa.: Reading Public Museum and Art Gallery. (29)

[160] * _____. 1946. "Cruising the Eastern Woods With a Delaware Chief." *Pennsylvania Archaeologist* 16:31-33.    (44)

[161]    _____. 1946. "The Delaware Indians as Women: Were the Original Pennsylvanians Politically Emasculated?" *Pennsylvania Magazine of History and Biography* 70: 377-389.    (23)

[162] * Stewart, Frank H. 1932. *Indians of Southern New Jersey. Publications of the Gloucester County Historical Society* 3. Woodbury, N.J.    (13)

[163] * Stewart, Tyrone. 1973. "Oklahoma Delaware Woman's Dance Clothes." *American Indian Crafts and Cultures* 7:4-13; 18-22.    (36)

[164]    Stone, Frederick D. 1882. "Penn's Treaty with the Indians, Did it Take Place in 1682 or 1683?" *Pennsylvania Magazine of History and Biography* 6:217-238.    (21)

[165]    Tantaquidgeon, Gladys. 1950. "Delaware Indian Art Designs." *Pennsylvania Archaeologist* 20:24-30.    (36)

[166]    _____. 1972. *Folk Medicine of the Delaware and Related Agonkian Indians.*

Pennsylvania Historical and Museum Commission. (A reprint of the author's *A Study of Delaware Indian Medicine Practice and Folk Beliefs*, Pennsylvania Historical Commission, 1942, with additional notes on Mohegan medical practice and folklore.)　　　(41)

[167]　Thompson, Charles N. 1937. *Sons of the Wilderness, John and William Conner*. *Indiana Historical Society Publications* 12. Indianapolis.　　　(29)

[168]　Thomson, Charles. 1759. *An Enquiry into the Causes of the Alienation of the Delaware and Shawanese Indians from the British Interest, and into the Measures taken for recovering their Friendship*. London: J. Wilkie. (Reprinted 1867, Philadelphia: John Campbell.)　　　(22)

[169]　Thornbrough, Gayle, ed. 1961. *Letter Book of the Indian Agency at Fort Wayne 1809-1815*. *Indiana Historical Society Publications* 21. Indianapolis.　　　(30)

[170]　Thwaites, Reuben G., and Louise P. Kellogg eds. 1908. *The Revolution on the Upper Ohio, 1775-1777*. Madison: Wisconsin Historical Society.　　　(27)

[171]　————. 1912. *Frontier Defense on the Upper Ohio, 1777-1778*. Madison: Wisconsin Historical Society.　　　(27)

[172]   Trelease, Allen W. 1960. *Indian Affairs in Colonial New York: The Seventeenth Century*. Ithaca: Cornell University Press.   (18)

[173]   Trowbridge, Charles C. [c. 1823] "Account of Some of the Traditions, Manners and Customs of the Lenee Lenaupaa or Delaware Indians." In C. A. Weslager, *The Delaware Indians, A History*. See No. 213, below.   (24)

[174]   "Two Minute Books of Kansas Missions in the Forties." 1933. *Kansas Historical Quarterly* 2:227-250.   (32)

[175]   Van der Donck, Adriaen. 1841. "A Description of the New Netherlands, [2nd Dutch edition 1656]." Trans. Jeremiah Johnson. *Collections of the New-York Historical Society*, 2nd series, 1:125-242. (First edition probably published in Amsterdam in 1653. Reprinted 1977, ed. Thomas F. O'Donnell Syracuse University Press.)

[176]   Vaux, Roberts. 1826. "A Memoir on the Locality of the Great Treaty Between William Penn and the Indian Natives [Delawares] in 1682." *Memoirs of the Historical Society of Pennsylvania* 1:81-98.   (21)

[177]    Voegelin, Charles F. 1940. "The
         Lenape and Munsee Dialects of Dela-
         ware, An Algonquian Language." *Pro-
         ceedings of the Indiana Academy of Science*
         49:34-37.                                    (39)

[178]    _____. 1941. "Word Distortions in
         Delaware Big House and Walam Olum
         Songs." *Proceedings of the Indiana Aca-
         demy of Science* 51:48-54.                   (39)

[179]    _____. 1946. "Delaware, an Eastern
         Algonquian Language." *Viking Fund
         Publications in Anthropology* 6: 130-157.
         New York.                                    (39)

[180]    Voegelin, Erminie W. 1939. "Culture
         Parallels to the Delaware Walam
         Olum." *Proceedings of the Indiana Aca-
         demy of Science* 49:29-31. (This article
         was expanded into a full chapter en-
         titled "Parallels to the Delaware Walam
         Olum," and published in 1954 in
         *Walam Olum, or Red Score: The Migration
         Legend of the Lenni Lenape or Delaware
         Indians*. See No. 184, below.                (7)

[181] *  Volkman, Arthur G. 1946. "Chief
         Naaman-Naaman Creek." *Bulletin of the
         Archaeological Society of Delaware* 4, no.
         3, pp. 2-8.                                  (42)

[182] * _____. 1949. "Lenape Basketry in Delaware." *Bulletin of the Archaeological Society of Delaware* 4, no. 5, pp. 15-18.    (42)

[183]   Wainwright, Nicholas B. 1959. *George Croghan, Wilderness Diplomat*. Published for the Institute of Early American History and Culture. Chapel Hill: University of North Carolina Press.    (26)

[184]   *Walam Olum, or Red Score: The Migration Legend of the Lenni Lenape or Delaware Indians*. 1954. Charles F. Voegelin, trans. Contributions by Eli Lilly, Erminie W. Voegelin, Joe E. Pierce, Glenn A. Black, Georg K. Newmann, 2nd, Paul Weer. Indianapolis: Indiana Historical Society.    (6, 45, 47)

[185]   Wallace, Anthony F. C. 1947. "Women, Land and Society: Three Aspects of Aboriginal Delaware Life." *Pennsylvania Archaeologist* 17:1-35.    (23)

[186]   _____. 1949. "The Role of the Bear in Delaware Society." *Pennsylvania Archaeologist* 19:37-46.    (29)

[187]   _____. 1949. *King of the Delawares: Teedyuscung, 1700-1763*. Philadelphia: University of Pennsylvania Press.    (26)

[188]   _____. 1950. "Some Psychological Characteristics of the Delaware Indians

During the 17th and 18th Centuries." *Pennsylvania Archaeologist* 20: 33-39. (15)

[189] ———. 1956. "New Religions Among the Delaware Indians, 1600-1900." *Southwest Journal of Anthropology* 12:1-21. (38)

[190] Wallace, Paul A. W. 1952. "John Heckewelder's Indians and the Fenimore Cooper Tradition." *Proceedings of the American Philosophical Society* 96:496-504. (37)

[191] ———. ed. 1958. *Thirty Thousand Miles with John Heckewelder*. Pittsburgh: University of Pittsburgh Press. (37)

[192] ———. 1960. "The John Heckewelder Papers." *Pennsylvania History* 27: 249-262. (37)

[193] * ———. 1961. *Indians in Pennsylvania*. Harrisburg: Pennsylvania Historical and Museum Commission. (19)

[194] ———. 1965. *Indian Paths of Pennsylvania*. Harrisburg: Pennsylvania Historical and Museum Commission. (19)

[195] Weer, Paul. 1947. "Thomas Dean and the Delaware Towns." *Proceedings of the Indiana Academy of Science* 56:26-32. (31)

[196]    Weslager, C.A. 1942. "Delaware Indian
         Villages." *Pennsylvania Archaeologist*
         12:53-56.                                    (10)

[197]    _____. 1943. "The Minquas and their
         Early Relations with the Delaware Indi-
         ans." *Bulletin of the Archaeological Society
         of Delaware* 4, no. 1, pp. 14-23.            (18)

[198] *  _____. 1944. *Delaware's Buried Past*,
         Philadelphia: University of Pennsyl-
         vania Press. (Reissued with an adden-
         dum 1968. New Brunswick, New Jer-
         sey, Rutgers University Press.)              (45)

[199]    _____. 1944. "The Delaware Indians
         as Women." *Journal of the Washington
         Academy of Sciences* 34:381-388.            (22)

[200]    _____. 1947. "Further Light on the
         Delaware Indians as Women." *Journal
         of the Washington Academy of Sciences*
         37:298-304.                                  (23)

[201]    _____. 1949. "The Indians of Lewes,
         Delaware, and an Unpublished Indian
         Deed Dated June 7, 1659." *Bulletin of
         the Archaeological Society of Delaware* 4,
         no. 5, pp. 6-14.                             (14)

[202]    _____ in collaboration with Arthur A.
         Dunlap. 1950. *Indian Place-Names in
         Delaware*. Wilmington: Archaeological
         Society of Delaware.                         (6)

[203] * ———. 1953. *A Brief Account of the Indians of Delaware*. Newark, Delaware: University of Delaware Press. (Second edition revised by author, reprinted in 1973.) (15)

[204] * ———. 1953. *Red Men on the Brandywine*. Wilmington: Hambleton Co. (Reissued with an addendum 1976, Wilmington: Delmarva News Agency, Inc.) (12)

[205] ———. 1954. "Robert Evelyn's Indian Tribes and Place Names of New Albion." *Bulletin of the Archaeological Society of New Jersey* 9:1-14. (12)

[206] ———. 1955. "The Delaware Indians, Their Gods, Their Religious Ceremonies." *Bulletin of the Archaeological Society of Delaware* 7, no. 1, pp. 31-38. (35)

[207] ———. 1956. "Delaware Indian Villages at Philadelphia." *Pennsylvania Archaeologist* 26:178-180. (10)

[208] * ———. 1957. "The Swede Meets the Red Man." *Bulletin of the Archaeological Society of Delaware* 8, no. 1, pp. 1-12. (9)

[209] ———, in collaboration with Arthur A. Dunlap. 1958. "Toponomy of the Delaware Valley as Revealed by an Early Seventeenth Century Dutch Map." *Bulletin of the Archaeological Soci-*

*ety of New Jersey*, No. 15-16, pp. 1-13.
(Includes facsimile of map showing In-
dian settlements.)                                      (12)

[210]    ———. 1961. *Dutch Explorers, Traders
and Settlers in the Delaware Valley, 1609-
1664*. Philadelphia: University of Penn-
sylvania Press.                                         (11)

[211]    ———, in collaboration with Arthur A.
Dunlap. 1961. "Names and Places in an
Unrecorded Delaware Indian Deed
(1681)" *Delaware History* 9:282-292.

[212]    ———. 1971. "Name-Giving Among
the Delaware Indians." *Names* 19:268-
283.                                                    (41)

[213]    ———. 1972. *The Delaware Indians, A
History*. New Brunswick: Rutgers Uni-
versity Press.                                      (3, 24, 31)

[214]    ———. 1972. "A New Look at Brinton's Lenape-English Dictionary."
*Pennsylvania Archaeologist* 42, no. 4, pp.
23-25. [Although published in 1974 this
number was dated December 1972 to
fill a gap in the series.]                              (40)

[215] * ———. 1973. *Magic Medicines of the In-
dians*. Somerset, N.J.: Middle Atlantic
Press. (Reprinted New York: 1974.
New American Library.)                                  (41)

[216] ———. "Enrollment List of Chippewa and Delaware-Munsies Living in Franklin County, Kansas, May 31, 1900." *Kansas Historical Quarterly* 40:234-240. (33)

[217] ———. 1975. "More About the Unalachtigo." *Pennsylvania Archaeologist* 45, no. 3, pp. 40-44. (35)

[218] * ———. 1978. *The Delaware Indian Westward Migration, With the Texts of Two Manuscripts (1821-22) Responding to General Lewis Cass's Inquiries About Lenape Culture and Language.* Wallingford: Middle Atlantic Press. (30, 31)

[219] ——— and James A. Rementer. 1977. "American Indian Genealogy and a List of Names Bestowed by a Delaware Indian Name-Giver." *Pennsylvania Genealogical Magazine* 30:22-31. (41)

[220] * Witthoft, John. 1946. "The Grasshopper War in Lenape Land." *Pennsylvania Archaeologist* 16:91-94. (43)

[221] ———. 1965. *Indian Prehistory of Pennsylvania.* Harrisburg: Pennsylvania Historical and Museum Commission. (45)

[222] * Wright, Muriel H. 1951. *A Guide to the Indian Tribes of Oklahoma.* Norman: University of Oklahoma Press. (See pp.

145-155 for discussion of the Delawares.)                                                    (33)

[223]    Zeisberger, David. 1910. *History of the Northern American Indians [1779-1780]*. Eds. Archer Butler Hulbert and William Nathaniel Schwarze. In *Ohio Archaeological and Historical Quarterly* 19:1-189. (Reprinted AMS Press, Inc.)    (34)

[224]    ———. 1912. *The Diaries of Zeisberger Relating to the First Mission in the Ohio Basin [1767-1769]*. Eds. Archer Butler Hulbert and William Nathaniel Schwarze. *The Moravian Records* 2. In *Ohio Archaeological and Historical Quarterly* 21:1-125.                              (37)

The Newberry Library
Center for the History of the American Indian
Founding Director: D'Arcy McNickle
Director: Francis Jennings

Established in 1972 by the Newberry Library, in conjunction with the Committee on Institutional Cooperation of eleven midwestern universities, the Center makes the resources of one of America's foremost research libraries in the Humanities available to those interested in improving the quality and effectiveness of teaching American Indian history. The Newberry's collections include some 100,000 volumes on the history of the American Indian and offer specialized resources for studying historical aspects of Indian-White relations and Indian linguistics. The Center also assists Native Americans engaged in writing tribal histories and developing educational materials.

## ADVISORY COMMITTEE

### Chairman: Alfonso Ortiz

Robert F. Berkhofer
*University of Michigan*

Robert V. Dumont, Jr.
*Native American Educational Services/Antioch College;*
*Fort Peck Reservation*

Raymond D. Fogelson
*University of Chicago*

William T. Hagan
*State University of New York College, Fredonia*

Robert F. Heizer
*University of California Berkeley*

Nancy O. Lurie
*Milwaukee Public Museum*

Cheryl Metoyer
*University of California, Los Angeles*

N. Scott Momaday
*Stanford University*

Father Peter J. Powell
*St. Augustine Indian Center*

Father Paul Prucha, S.J.
*Marquette University*

Faith Smith
*Native American Educational Services/Antioch College;*
*Chicago*

Sol Tax
*University of Chicago*

Robert K. Thomas
*Wayne State University*

Robert M. Utley
*Advisory Council on Historical Preservation; Washington, D.C.*

Antoinette McNickle Vogel

Dave Warren
*Institute of American Indian Arts*

Wilcomb E. Washburn
*Smithsonian Institution*